To our dear friends
  Peter & Lorraine.
An aide memoire to all the
faceless ones, or should that be
multi-faced ones, who confused
everyone including themselves.
    Enjoy.

Decline and Fail

DECLINE and FAIL

Read in Case of
Political Apocalypse

JOHN CRACE

This edition first published in the UK in 2019
by Guardian Books, Kings Place, 90 York Way, London N1 9GU
and Faber & Faber Ltd, Bloomsbury House,
74–77 Great Russell Street, London WC1B 3DA

Printed in the UK by CPI Group (UK) Ltd, Croydon CR0 4YY

Cover illustrations © Morten Morland, originally produced for the
Spectator

The right of John Crace to be identified as author of this work has been
asserted in accordance with Section 77 of the Copyright, Designs and
Patents Act 1988

A CIP record for this book is available from the British Library

ISBN 978–1–78335–193–0

FSC
www.fsc.org
MIX
Paper from
responsible sources
FSC® C020471

4 6 8 10 9 7 5 3

For Anna and Robert

Introduction

Theresa May took office in July 2016 with one job and one job only. To deliver Brexit. But there was a problem with this. The two Leave campaigns had been very careful not to define exactly what Brexit meant in order to maximise their appeal. Some had voted to leave because they wanted less immigration, others had voted for the UK to regain its sovereignty from the EU. Some were openly relaxed about the UK remaining in the single market and the customs union, others demanded nothing less than a clean break from all EU institutions.

So there was no clear roadmap to Brexit and it was up to May, whom many commentators had confidently declared to be a safe pair of hands, a competent bureaucrat, to set her own vision. Which she did by repeatedly stating that Brexit meant Brexit. At first this was received as some kind of mystic vision, loaded with wisdom, but it wasn't long before many people began to wonder if there was less to May than met the eye. And when she started uttering sentences, such as 'I am determined to deliver on the things which I am determined to deliver', her characterisation as the Maybot was born.

1

By January 2017, many of the Brexiteers in the Conservative party were beginning to get decidedly twitchy. It was seven months since the referendum and the UK had made no real moves to leave the EU. Nor was it at all clear on what terms we would be leaving. Not least because the EU had itself refused to enter any discussions with the UK on the divorce settlement and any future trade agreement until after Article 50 was triggered. So eventually, Theresa May was forced to jump. Having decided that alienating the hardline Eurosceptic MPs of the European Research Group risked splitting the Tory party – on balance, she rightly considered her Remainer-leaning MPs to be more amenable and pliable – she delivered a speech at Lancaster House that spelled out what Brexit actually meant. No membership of the single market or a customs union and no jurisdiction by the European Court of Justice. A hard Brexit.

Parliament voted to trigger Article 50 on March 29th. The die had been cast. The UK had laid out its Brexit objectives and had set in motion the two-year time limit in which to achieve it. This was the high point of the May administration and she was widely praised by many sections of the media as the prime minister who had stood up to Europe and delivered on the result of the referendum. This period of grace lasted only a matter of weeks.

In the first nine months of her premiership, May had been explicitly asked seven times on national television whether she would be calling a general election. On each

2

occasion she had said no, insisting it wouldn't be in the national interest. After a brief walking holiday in Wales, she returned to Downing Street after the Easter break and promptly declared a general election. The calculation was quite straightforward. The Conservatives were about 20 points ahead of Labour in the opinion polls and on course for a majority of between 80 and 100 seats. Enough for her to wipe out the opposition for a generation and to force any deal through parliament without having to worry about the Brexit hardliners in her own party.

Where the strategy fell apart was in the execution. First her advisers encouraged her to run a presidential-style campaign. Not the most obvious choice for a prime minister with little charisma or personality who had made plain she intended to avoid all TV debates. Then May was forced to disown her own manifesto after her dementia tax was universally panned. With the prime minister in full meltdown – even the right-wing press were now calling her the Maybot – unable to do more than repeat 'Strong and Stable' and 'Nothing has Changed' while looking perpetually startled, and with Jeremy Corbyn campaigning rather more passionately than he had in the referendum, the polls began to narrow.

Even so, it was a major shock – not just to the Conservatives, but also to Labour – when the result of the June general election was declared and May had lost her overall majority. If the election had been a proxy vote on Brexit, then the country was every bit as divided *as it had been the year before. The prime minister had gambled and lost. She returned to Downing Street with her position far weaker than before and relying on the votes – thanks to a £1 billion bung – on the 10 MPs of the Northern Irish Democratic Unionist Party.*

From then on, May was firmly on the back foot. She retired to lick her wounds over the summer and her attempt to reassert her authority over her party with the party conference speech in the autumn ended in excruciating embarrassment. First a protestor presented her with a P45. Then she lost her voice. Then parts of the scenery collapsed around her. May's world was literally collapsing around her.

Meanwhile the EU looked on in amazement. There had always been a very good reason why the EU had made Article 50 a two-year process. Because it had imagined most countries would conclude it was an impossibly short time in which to agree a settlement and therefore not worth doing. Predictably the EU chose to make the process as difficult as possible by insisting that it would refuse to discuss the future trading relationships before citizens' rights, the divorce bill and the Irish border had been agreed. Something to which the UK had little choice other than to agree.

If things were going badly in Brussels – citizens' rights and a £39 billion divorce bill were eventually agreed, but Ireland proved a whole lot trickier as the DUP were unwilling to sign off anything that treated Northern

Ireland differently to the rest of the UK – they were also crumbling back in the UK. David Davis, the Brexit secretary, had claimed his department had produced 57 sectoral assessments analysing Brexit's potential impact in 'excruciating detail', but when parliament called his bluff and demanded to see them, they showed that the UK was hopelessly underprepared.

The government was also falling apart, with three ministers being forced to resign. Michael Fallon and Damian Green for allegations of sexual misconduct and Priti Patel for lying about conducting her own unofficial foreign policy. With just a year left on the clock until the UK was to leave the EU, May's grasp on power was looking increasingly tenuous – and the country was no clearer on just what Brexit would really mean.

The sky won't fall in after Brexit? Maybe not for you, Theresa

29 MARCH 2018

There are few things more guaranteed to induce a sense of national panic than the prime minister announcing she is doing a whistle-stop tour of the country to reassure everyone that leaving the EU wasn't going to be quite as bad as they feared. To mark the year to go till Brexit day, Theresa May started out by spending a few minutes at a textile factory in Ayr. Shortly after she left, most of the workers were checking to see if the factory was about to close.

Quite why the prime minister puts herself and the nation through such ordeals is something of a mystery. She finds it hard enough to look one of her cabinet ministers in the eye and clearly feels even more uncomfortable meeting ordinary people. The feeling is mutual. Her smiles are more like gurns and her conversation is mostly notable for its silences. At her second stop of the day, she sucked the life out of a children's daycare centre in Northumberland and everyone breathed a sigh of relief when she headed off.

7

Next on the itinerary was Bangor in Northern Ireland, where she had a private lunch with four farmers. One of them was dragged out to discuss on Sky News how it felt to have drawn the short straw. The poor man looked totally traumatised by the experience as he described how the prime minister had done absolutely nothing to convince them that she had a solution to the Irish border question. Partly because she didn't have one, but also because she had barely said a word.

Some time en route, May found time to give an interview to the BBC's Laura Kuenssberg. Would she like to say what kind of Brexit dividend Britain would be getting? Not really, the prime minister shrugged, because there probably wasn't going to be one. Kuenssberg wasn't getting the feelgood story she had been expecting. She tried another tack. Will Brexit be worth it?

'I think Brexit is going to deliver a country that will be different,' the prime minister said carefully. Kuenssberg tried to get her to expand on the nature of this difference. 'I said the sky won't fall in,' May continued, her software close to crashing, 'but it will be different and it will be different.' She could hardly have sounded less enthusiastic about Brexit if she had tried. Off camera, her advisers were tearing their hair out. By the time she got back to London, even Jacob Rees-Mogg would be having second thoughts about the wisdom of leaving the EU.

The whole day might have gone rather better if the prime minister had stayed at home and sent Tony Blair out in her place. Instead the former Labour prime minister was to be found addressing a couple of hundred people at the UK in a Changing Europe conference where he laid out his Brexit agenda. Or Breggsit agenda, as he prefers to call it.

Blair's tragedy is that when he had the country's trust, he dealt too often in half-truths and lies: and now he's on the level, most of the country doesn't believe a word he says. So if he had been heard on the national news channels saying we needed to be realistic about our global standing – Britain was now only a medium-sized player that had benefited from being part of one of the world's biggest political alliances – then he would probably have convinced even the most ardent Remainers that the UK was heading to be a global superpower. Breggsit: bring it on. Just show us the cliff edge and we'll happily jump.

There we had it. A prime minister who doesn't believe in her own policies but is trying to persuade herself she does. And a former prime minister who did persuade himself he believed in what he was doing and now wishes he hadn't. The state of Britain. The state of us. Three hundred and sixty five days and counting.

Boorish Boris Johnson is now a one-man rogue state

15 MAY 2018

There was a time when the post of foreign secretary was considered one of the great offices of state. A person who could be guaranteed to remain calm under fire and take the heat out of global flashpoints. Someone other countries might take seriously and respect.

For reasons best known to itself, though, the Conservative government has abandoned any pretence of taking the foreign secretary seriously. Boris Johnson is now a one-man rogue state, free to do more or less exactly what he wants, safe in the knowledge that no one dares sack him. A latter-day Toby Young on speed who roams the world losing friends and alienating people at an alarming rate. His motto: there's no bad situation that can't be made worse.

Boris doesn't hold with anything so old-fashioned as diplomacy. His mission is not the promotion of peace, it is the tireless promotion of himself. In Boris world, nothing really matters but Boris. Anything and everything is just leverage for his own career. A walking narcissistic personality disorder, the last remaining believer in his own genius who is oblivious to the destruction he creates.

10

Even when confronted with a list of his more obvious failings at Foreign Office questions, Boris shows an almost psychopathic lack of remorse. The fact that Nazanin Zaghari-Ratcliffe faces extra charges as a result of his incompetence doesn't seem to cost him a second of sleep. And certainly not his job. In his own echo chamber of a mind, everything he does gets rewritten as a major triumph.

Take the Commonwealth. Even the doziest Brexiter MP knows that increased trade with the Commonwealth won't come anywhere close to making up for lost trade with the EU if the UK leaves the customs union and the single market, but Boris feels free to insist that it will.

And no one bothers to contradict him – mainly because it's not worth it. There's only so many times you can point out that a serial liar is lying before you want to kill yourself. So he jabbers and blathers on, laughing at his own tired jokes that no one else now finds funny.

Boris's selective memory has extended to all corners of the globe. He forgot that Malaysia's new 92-year-old prime minister is a committed antisemite when praising the return of democracy to that country. He forgot that he had once said President Erdoğan was the 'wankerer from Ankara', when welcoming the visit of the Turkish leader to the UK.

He forgot he had called for Donald Trump to be awarded the Nobel prize shortly before the US president pulled out of the Iran nuclear deal and moved his embassy from

Tel Aviv to Jerusalem. He forgot there is no area of real-politik that he can't be relied on to make the wrong call.

Labour's Emily Thornberry chose to test him on his recall of cabinet splits over the customs union. Did he think cameras counted as physical infrastructure? Silly question. Boris doesn't think. So he didn't answer. Would he care to explain his differences with the prime minister and how he thought his 'Mad Max' plans would work?

'I am completely behind our magnificent prime minister,' he declared. Even his most loyal fans on the Tory backbenches were taken aback at that. Boris didn't even so much as blush. If Theresa May had even a hint of self-worth she would sack him right now, before he undermines her any further. She'd feel so much better if she did. And so would the rest of us.

The Tories had wisely made sure that Boris was kept off the subject of the massacre of more than 50 Palestinians by the Israelis. Some things are too sensitive to be handled by the foreign secretary. So it was left to junior minister, Alistair Burt, to update the house.

What did he make of Boris's claims that the US moving its embassy could be a force for peace? 'I always agree with the foreign secretary,' he said miserably. At least there's one person left in government who still believes in collective responsibility.

Corbyn finds the formula to fire up the Maybot. Just ask after Brexit

16 MAY 2018

Jeremy Corbyn has a stubborn streak. Critics might call him a slow learner. But even he can recognise when he's on to a winning streak. After months – years – of rambling on about something sent in by Susan of Solihull that goes on for so long no one can remember quite what his original point was, the Labour leader has twigged that prime minister's questions isn't really that complicated. Especially when you're up against someone as hopeless as Theresa May.

Last week, Corbyn broke with the habit of a lifetime by asking six short questions about Brexit and had the best PMQs of his time as leader. So quite understandably, he opted for doing the same thing this week. With precisely the same result. At this rate Wednesdays could become a cushy number for the Labour leader. Why bother to spend hours mugging up on the NHS or Windrush, when all you need to do is casually inquire how the prime minister thinks Brexit is coming along and then sit back and wait for everyone to start sniggering.

'How is Brexit coming along?' Corbyn asked. Theresa was completely blindsided by this. As if she had never heard of Brexit, let alone had a solution to it. Her mouth opened and shut as she waited for her voice to synch with her lips. Umm, Brexit, she said, stalling for time as she willed an electrical charge to fire up her circuit board.

It had all been going so well that she had divided the cabinet subcommittee into two sub-subcommittees. One sub-subcommittee had said that everything was going splendidly because the solution they were working on was a complete waste of time. And the second sub-subcommittee that had been working on the other solution had reported that they, too, thought things couldn't be better because their option was a total non-starter.

To make things even clearer, the Northern Ireland secretary, Karen Bradley, had spent the morning telling the select committee that both solutions were equally workable. As in equally unworkable. Theresa was now minded to further divide the two sub-subcommittees into three sub-sub-subcommittees.

Corbyn then further confused the prime minister by asking her epistemological questions on the nature of friction. How much friction was as little friction as possible? 'The government has a policy,' the prime minister creaked, defaulting to her normal Maybot mode. A policy of having done almost nothing for two years. A policy of literally not having a clue.

Alongside the prime minister on the government front bench, there were collective groans of despair. The closest the cabinet has come to a show of unity in months. Even Matt Hancock, who has never knowingly met a bum he doesn't feel compelled to lick, threw his head back in a state of tortured rictus. Shares in the heroin trade rose sharply. At times like these, only oblivion will do.

The Maybot stumbled on. An incoherent death spiral of free association. The Art of Mindlessnessnessness. Failing to answer even the easiest questions. Failing even to realise that she had inadvertently committed the UK to remaining in the customs union. The ghost of Freud. It was terrifying to realise that someone whose job description is to speak and think is often incapable of doing either.

Corbyn merely stuck to his formula. Keep it simple, stupid. It didn't really matter that his own party's position is inconsistent with the realities of Brexit. Labour doesn't have to come up with any intelligent ideas of its own. It merely has to point out the stupidity of the government's. AKA shooting fish in a barrel. The hunt for the cabinet's solitary brain cell continues.

There was some light relief when the Tory MP, Owen Paterson, who is just out of hospital after falling off a horse, intervened. What Paterson had learned from his mishap was that the horse had been a Remainer saboteur and that everyone in the hospital in which he had been treated had come round to thinking Brexit was a good idea when threatened with deportation. His injuries may have been more severe than first thought. The Maybot smiled gratefully. It was always nice to know there was someone more delusional than her.

At prime minister's questions on 6 June, Jeremy Corbyn asked if the government was going to publish its long-delayed white paper on its negotiating position before the Commons voted on the Lords' amendments to the Brexit withdrawal the following week. As it might be quite handy. If not essential for anyone hoping to make an informed decision.

May struggled for words. She agreed that the white paper might be a good idea, but there was a snag. The cabinet could not agree what should be in it. Or when it should be published. The white paper remained defiantly white.

As a metaphor for Brexit the actual debate on the Lords amendments could hardly have been bettered. A speech cut off in mid-sentence due to an arbitrary time limit set by the government, and the chief whip darting around the chamber desperately pleading with Tory rebels not to defeat the government over a meaningful vote.

The solicitor general making up government policy on the hoof while making plea bargain concessions in public to Dominic Grieve. A government that can barely negotiate with itself, let alone the EU. Hundreds of MPs milling around, unsure of what had and hadn't been agreed. The rebels reckoned they had a deal, while a government minister briefed that they had been stitched up. A shambles. AKA strong and stable leadership in the national interest.

The session ended in chaos. Anna Soubry appeared suspicious, but Grieve reassured her they were going to get what they wanted. Almost immediately, prominent Brexiters were claiming they wouldn't. Not for the first time May appeared to have promised different things to both sides. Indecision and ambivalence are the only things at which she excels. But something had to give. And it was going to get messy.

Don't panic! Brexit Dad's Army ready and willing to tell EU to sod off

14 JUNE 2018

The Royal Mail has done some expert trolling this week by announcing plans to release a set of *Dad's Army* stamps. 'Don't panic! Don't panic!' and 'We're all doomed!' might be just the kind of nostalgic messages being whispered within the government but ministers are keen not to let the good news spread to members of the general public. Careless talk costs lives and all that.

There was some good news for the Brexit department. The Royal Mail stopped short of superimposing the heads of ministers on those of the Walmington-on-Sea Home Guard. David Davis is the perfect Captain Mainwaring.

17

All mouth and no trousers, the perfect leader for any dis-organised retreat: the bank manager capable of mis-selling himself his own pension.

Then there's Steve Baker, the spivvy Private Walker. A man to flog the country a dodgy Brexit straight off the back of a lorry. Preferably one parked up on the M2 outside Dover. Robin Walker, the very essence of Private Pike. Nice but dim. Too stupid to appreciate the irony in his constant repetition of Brexit Britain wanting 'the brightest and the best'. If that was really the case, Walker wouldn't have a job.

Suella Braverman is slightly more of a problem. There weren't many women in Dad's Army and she would be an unlikely contender to be Pike's mother. But with a stretch of the imagination she could pass for Private Godfrey. Someone whose grasp on reality is increasingly slim and who largely exists in a private fantasy world where people losing their jobs is a price worth paying for the One True Brexit.

It was Walker – the spiv rather than the Robin – who got Brexit questions in the Commons under way in characteristic fashion. Britain had an unwavering com-mitment to workers' rights, he said, but if it turned out that those commitments weren't quite as unwavering as he promised then it was just one of those things. This was music to the ears of Tory Brexiters who have been getting a bit twitchy in recent weeks. David TC Davies jumped up to check that we would still be able to tell the EU to sod off. The spiv was happy to confirm it wouldn't be just the EU we would tell to sod off. It would be the whole world.

Next over the top were Privates Pike and Godfrey. Pike was happy to confirm that making up policy in real time during the debate on the meaningful vote earlier in the week was precisely the sort of tactic that struck fear into the enemy. If we didn't know what we were doing then there was little chance of the EU second-guessing us. Godfrey went one further by refusing to recognise anything she didn't like. Her own department's best-case scenario indicating that Scotland would be 2.9% worse off after Brexit was just wrong. The foreign secretary's remarks that the Brexit negotiations were a mess were unpatriotic.

Leading from the rear was Captain Mainwaring, bravely karate-chopping away all comers. First he saw off Hilary Benn. It wasn't true that Michel Barnier had rejected the government's idiotic Northern Ireland Brexit backstop plan as idiotic. What Barnier had actually done was to say he would reject the idiotic backstop plan as idiotic in a week or so's time when the EU Council next met.

Mainwaring smiled to himself, thrilled at the brilliance of his own logic. A few of the sharper minds in the house started sobbing. Jacob Rees-Mogg made a mental note to transfer the administration of more of his trust funds to Ireland. Keir Starmer then chose to take one for the country. Observing that the Brexit secretary had threatened to resign more often than he had met with Barnier over the last six months, he asked for clarification over

19

the meaningful vote. Who was going to win? Dominic Grieve or the solicitor general?

'The solicitor general,' said Mainwaring confidently. It was vital for the sovereignty of parliament that parliament should not be sovereign. You couldn't risk this taking back control business falling into the wrong hands.

Starmer ran the same question by the minister again. This time Mainwaring gave an entirely different answer. He had no idea what was going to be in the amendment that was due to be tabled later in the afternoon, so everyone would have to wait and see. A self-satisfied nod. He hadn't got where he was today by knowing what he was doing.

* * *

Not for the first time, Boris Johnson had done himself no favours. First he had needed to arrange an entirely pointless day trip to Afghanistan at the taxpayer's expense to save himself the embarrassment of wondering whether to keep his promise to vote against the government over the Heathrow expansion and resign as foreign secretary. The battle between cowardice and principle is almost invariably a losing one for Johnson.

Then he had been recorded saying 'Fuck business' – a sentiment that had gone down like a cup of cold sick in the Tory party – and prompted many leading multinational companies to question the government's competence in its handling of Brexit. Still, the one piece of good news for Theresa May was that the men's World Cup had started and most of the country would be spending the next month more preoccupied with football than politics.

Napping May scores own goal in face of Belgium Brexit striker

28 JUNE 2018

Not even catching a glimpse of Iain Duncan Smith in the *Daily Mail* cleverly comparing British business to Nazi collaborators – irony meters went off the scale – could spoil Theresa May's morning. Flying to Brussels was the prime minister's very own 'me time'. A time when she could put her feet up and no one or nothing could get to her for an hour or so. Several members of her cabinet could have launched blue-on-blue attacks. One or two might even have resigned. And she would be none the wiser. Which is just the way she liked it.

Life was about to get better still. Her two-day visit to the European Council was about to merge into a four-day weekend because she literally had nothing to do. The summit was meant to be the time when the prime minister spelled out the final details of Britain's withdrawal agreement with the EU but what with one thing and another – mainly her incompetence and cluelessness – this had been pushed back yet again.

She was now hoping she would be in a position to announce the terms of the withdrawal six months after Britain had withdrawn. So she could sit back, kick off her shoes and let the other EU leaders rabbit on. They might all get round to discussing Brexit once she had left, but it worked better for everyone that way. It was the only way any progress could be guaranteed.

Shortly after landing, May stopped off for a coffee. It was customary to let the more important EU leaders turn up first, so she had time to kill and could watch them arrive on TV. There were Emmanuel Macron and Angela Merkel embracing one another. May felt a small pang of sadness. There was a time when she might have been a member of the inner circle. There again, she wasn't even a member of the inner circle in her cabinet any more.

A little later, the Dutch prime minister, Mark Rutte, appeared and gave a mini press conference. After talking about immigration, he was asked for his thoughts on how Brexit was progressing. 'I don't want to say it's apocalyptic but . . .' he said. But it was apocalyptic. Next came the Irish taoiseach, Leo Varadkar. 'We had been expecting progress . . . any progress,' he said unhelpfully. Was Britain really being serious in its negotiations. 'We'll have to wait and see.' If there had been anything left alive in Theresa, it too would have died at that point.

Then the prime minister got the nod. There was a spare five minutes on the red carpet if she wanted to use it. May wandered purposefully towards the only microphone that wasn't switched on so her opening words went unrecorded. Eventually the sound cut in and she could be heard saying how happy she was that the summit was prioritising the prohibition of chemical weapons. Everyone looked blank. They had imagined immigration was the main subject up for discussion.

Next came the Brexit question. 'We are making very good progress,' said May. The blank faces turned even blanker. What did she imagine little progress would look like? A reporter pointed out that wasn't what the other EU leaders were saying. 'We've been setting things out,' she babbled desperately. 'We're in a strong position . . . we want to sit down and move at pace.' A snail's pace.

Once inside the main hall, the Belgian prime minister, Charles Michel, made a beeline for the prime minister. Pulling a Belgian football shirt out of his bag, he thrust it into May's hands. Which she promptly held up for the cameras. Half time: Belgium 1 (May og), England 0.

'Oh look,' she said. 'It's got a Number 10 on it. I live at Number 10. What a coincidence! Are Belgium playing tonight?'

Michel couldn't believe his luck and started distributing Belgium scarves to everyone else. Jean-Claude Juncker held his above his head. So, too, did Varadkar. Before long the whole room was pointing at the prime minister and chanting, 'You're shit and you know you are; you're shit, and you know you are.' Final score: Belgium 27, England 0.

* * *

On Friday 6th July, Theresa May summoned her entire cabinet to Chequers, the prime minister's Buckinghamshire weekend home, to agree the Brexit plan she proposed to offer the EU. Phones were confiscated at the door and ministers were warned that anyone who didn't feel able to sign up to the deal would be expected to resign and return home by cab. Business cards with the telephone number of a local taxi firm were helpfully left out on a table by the front door.

After ten hours of talks, May's hardball tactics of trying to bounce the more hardline Brexiteers in her government into coming on board with her deal appeared to have paid off. The cabinet all signed off an agreement committing the UK to maintaining a close relationship with the EU. There would be continued access to the single market for goods and a common rulebook on state aid, forbidding government subsidies of particular industries.

May also stated there would be no hard border between Northern Ireland and the Republic of Ireland and no border in the UK. An as yet not fully specified 'facilitated customs arrangement' would remove the need for checks between the UK and the EU. At the conclusion of the talks, Boris Johnson promised to write a newspaper opinion piece endorsing the deal and urging Eurosceptics to put aside their misgivings and get behind it. Number 10 declared that collective

24

responsibility was up and running again after months of disunity.

That last claim didn't age well. Within hours of the deal being announced, it was being attacked by both Remainer and Leaver Tory MPs. The former believed it a fudge that would leave the UK worse off than it was inside the bloc; the latter saw it as a betrayal. Both Labour and the Lib Dems predicted that the prime minister's deal would never get past her own party, let alone parliament. The EU was similarly lukewarm in its response. Michel Barnier welcomed the fact that the UK had finally come up with some kind of proposal – better late than never – but other EU leaders were sceptical, arguing that May had failed to grasp that the UK was not in a position to cherry-pick which bits of the EU it liked. Ultimately any deal would have to be determined by the red lines that she herself had laid down in her Lancaster House speech more than a year previously.

Two days later, Brexit secretary David Davis resigned saying he couldn't support the deal. The next day, Boris Johnson followed suit, not wanting to be left out of the Brexiteer in-crowd. So brave. Quite why it took both men so long to realise that they actually disagreed with the thing they had wholeheartedly endorsed just days earlier is anyone's guess. Perhaps the threat of the cab ride home from Chequers had been effective. Davis was replaced by Dominic Raab. Jeremy Hunt was moved from the department of health to become foreign secretary.

Why does Theresa May hate making decisions? Because they all go wrong

9 JULY 2018

It's now clear why Theresa May is so averse to making decisions. On the rare occasions she does come up with a plan, it invariably seems to go hopelessly wrong. Surprising her cabinet with a new Brexit customs plan that nobody else had seen and daring any ministers who disagreed with it to resign and take the taxi ride of shame home from Chequers had initially seemed to pay off.

There was a rare burst of cabinet unanimity over the weekend with everyone admitting they were taken aback that the prime minister had actually done something.

Then the surprise wore off and, just before midnight on Sunday, the Brexit secretary chose to resign, conceding that he wasn't the right person to implement the prime minister's vision of Brexit. Most people wondered what had taken David Davis so long. He had never been the right person to deliver anyone's vision of Brexit.

Midway through Monday afternoon, having holed himself up in his official residence and failed to attend a west Balkans summit he was due to host that had been designed to display Britain's post-Brexit openness, Boris Johnson belatedly offered his own resignation as foreign secretary. After years of fruitless searching, he had finally found a principle he could get behind. His career. To have stayed on after Davis had jumped ship would have made him look even more spineless than usual.

Half an hour later, and with a couple of hasty rewrites to recast the disintegration of her government as natural wastage, May went to the Commons to give a statement on why she was the only person in Britain who believed her 'facilitated customs arrangement' was a plausible solution. She cast her eye around the chamber. Dominic Raab was on the front bench. At least he hadn't got round to resigning yet.

There was no sign of Davis and Johnson, so there was no danger of a Geoffrey Howe attack. And then Michael Gove slipped in just as she got to her feet. If he was planning to jump ship, he wasn't going to do so today. All was about as good as it could be. She would survive.

May began first by damning Davis and Johnson with faint praise. Davis had been totally exhausted by the four hours of negotiations he had completed with Michel Barnier during his time in office; Boris needed time alone after years of shameless self-promotion.

She then went on to explain her magical thinking. Her customs arrangement was going to deliver both the hard Brexit that the right wing of her party had demanded and the soft Brexit that business and everyone else in the country was begging for. We would be in and out of the customs union, the single market and the European Court of Justice. 'What we are preparing is challenging for the EU,' she declared to widespread laughter. It was also challenging for anyone with half a functioning synapse.

As so often when faced with the government in a near terminal death spiral, Jeremy Corbyn decided that the best course of action for the opposition was not to oppose. Instead of showing leadership by coming up with any clear alternative of his own, he just shouted out a few obvious objections before getting into competitive boasting with the prime minister over which of them would have conducted the fewest preparations before triggering article 50. 'It's me.' 'No, it's me.' May looked at him with a look that came close to love. At times like these, the Labour leader is her closest ally in the Commons. Somewhere there is an eighth circle of hell in which they are a couple.

Thereafter the session divided down predictable lines. Tory Brexiters, such as Iain Duncan Smith, Owen Paterson, Jacob Rees-Mogg and Andrea Jenkyns, voiced their disquiet over the prime minister's deal while Remainers, such as Anna Soubry and Nicky Morgan, congratulated May on her leadership – they just about managed not to snigger – in facing down the hardliners. Even if her deal was a bit rubbish.

For her part, May was content to cruise on auto-pilot. She could do being a bit useless and saying one thing to one person and another to someone else in her sleep. It was what she was programmed to do.

It took the Labour backbenchers to give the prime minister a reality check. Ben Bradshaw startled everyone by declaring that he believed May 'to be a rational human being'. No one else does. Barry Sheerman urged her to escape the imprisonment of the far right of her party. May adopted the persona of someone in a hostage video and insisted: 'I am acting of my own accord'. If true, that would make the situation even more terrifying.

Wes Streeting pointed out that even if her deal wasn't useless – which it was – the government didn't have the numbers to get it through parliament. May stuck her fingers in her ears and yelled, 'La, la, la'. Yvette Cooper had another go. Could the prime minister not see she was again saying 'nothing has changed' when everything had changed. Apart from the fact that this deal, like all the others, was dead in the water. 'I didn't say nothing has changed,' the prime minister said. 'I said it had evolved a bit.' But nothing had changed. May was still a bit hopeless. And still waiting on a miracle.

Who runs the country? The answer is too awful to contemplate

16 JULY 2018

'Nothing has changed, nothing has changed,' a fragile Theresa May snapped during her statement on the NATO

29

summit, after Labour's Stephen Kinnock had observed she had effectively ripped up her own Chequers white paper by accepting the wrecking amendments to her customs bill that had been tabled by the hardline Brexiters of the European Reform Group.

She was right. Nothing had changed. Yet again, when faced with a challenge to her authority from the right wing of her party, she had given way. May is a psyche in near total collapse. Someone whose only remaining function is to try to do whatever it takes get through to the end of each day in the hope that tomorrow never comes. A prime minister in name only.

That thought was uppermost in Anna Soubry's mind when she opened the debate on the third reading of the customs bill. Who was running the country, she asked? Theresa May or Jacob Rees-Mogg? The answer was even more terrifying than the question. The reality is that no one appears to be running the country. At a time when the UK is in the grip of a political and existential crisis, the government is no more than flotsam drifting aimlessly between competing tides of reality and ideology.

Soubry was damning of her ERG colleagues on the Tory benches and forensic in her dismantling of their arguments, accusing them of putting hundreds of thousands of jobs at risk when they were protected by gold-plated pensions and private incomes. This predictably drew return blue-on-blue fire from the ERG cabal of Edward Leigh,

Christopher 'Upskirting' Chope, David Davis, Steve Baker, Priti Patel and Bernard Jenkin who were huddled together near the back of the chamber. A true confederacy of dunces. Six MPs in search of a brain cell.

'You ain't no Margaret Thatcher,' leered Leigh in, what was for him, one of his more intelligent contributions to parliamentary life. Even his colleagues appeared embarrassed by that. All but Jenkin, who was hellbent on seeing how high he could raise the stupidity bar. Having earlier in the day declared that business was far too interested in making money, he now suggested that the way to reconcile just-in-time production with longer border checks was to make sure that lorries set out from the EU several days earlier than they currently did. That way it wouldn't matter if they got held up. If he wasn't already an MP, Jenkin would be hard pushed to get a job.

Often in the past, Soubry has been more talk than action. She labours under the misapprehension that it's possible to fight the ideology of a hard Brexit with appeals to reason. So when she agreed to withdraw her own amendment to remain in the customs union to show willing, the Brexiters just sniggered at the back. They thought that yet again she and the other Remainers were ineffectual if noisy cheerleaders. This time though, they appeared to have found some steel. The Remainer rebels had finally learned how to rebel. For the government, it was another unnecessary self-inflicted wound. A total clusterfuck.

Moments later, Davis stood up to make his first contribution in the house since his resignation last week. He opened by saying he wasn't going to make a Geoffrey Howe-style resignation speech rubbishing the prime minister. Rather he wanted to go out of his way to offer an olive branch. Now that May had officially abandoned her Chequers agreement there was nothing to stop her reappointing him as Brexit secretary. Let bygones be bygones. If May could pretend that nothing had happened – or indeed changed – then so could he. The year of magical thinking.

What Davis hadn't banked on was his own intellect. Or lack of it. In making a pitch for wisdom, he unwittingly proved exactly why he had always been so unsuited to being in office. Not so much gravitas, as levitas. The best way to increase world trade was to trash our trade with the EU. We needed lorries to be stacked up outside Dover. Hard borders? No problem. Best of all, we were bound to get a great trade deal because as the other EU countries couldn't speak English they wouldn't be able to understand when we were negotiating in English. Really.

He was heard in near silence by MPs on both sides of the house. Under the circumstances it was the kindest response. Davis is now a stranger not just to government but also to intelligent life.

Yet again nothing had changed.

Boris Johnson's fans wanted a roaring lion. They got a paper tiger

18 JULY 2018

His departure became his time in office. Long on bombast, short on content. Long on grandiosity, short on self-awareness. In public and in private, Boris Johnson is a disappointment. Not least to himself. Cut through the fragile narcissism and there is a ball of self-loathing and insecurity. No one understands his own failure better than him. A man of little courage and fewer principles. The lion that keeps forgetting to roar.

Never one to pass up an opportunity to manoeuvre himself into the history books, Boris had chosen almost the identical seat in the Commons to make his resignation speech as Geoffrey Howe had taken for his in 1990. There the comparisons ended.

Howe had been addressing the prime minister in person. Boris was speaking mainly to himself. Theresa May was otherwise engaged with an appearance before the liaison committee, and the government had managed to programme so much pointless prior business that most other MPs had drifted away.

So the chamber was only about a third full for his statement. And, apart from a small handful of Boris Believers that included Nadine Dorries, Ben Bradley and

33

David Davis, most were only there out of idle curiosity. To be there at the end of a career that had promised much but delivered little. Howe's speech had done for Margaret Thatcher. Boris succeeded only in doing for himself.

He began by thanking the staff of the Foreign Office for all their hard work while he was in charge. The gratitude hadn't been reciprocated. When Boris had resigned, some in the Foreign Office had broken out the champagne. They were thrilled to be finally rid of the worst foreign secretary in living memory.

He then moved on to the prime minister. Theresa was a marvellous woman. Full of resilience. Absolutely the best woman for the job. If only she were completely different. As so often with Boris, his speech was a model of disingenuousness. He might have imagined it to be oratory, but everyone else could see it for its hollowness. And cowardice. Even when he was questioning May's authority, he couldn't bring himself to do so directly.

What followed was a leadership challenge by innuendo. Boris couldn't even bring himself to take ownership of his own actions. A man for whom opportunism and disloyalty is so innate, he cannot prevent himself from being disloyal to himself. The words flowed easily enough, but they were nearly all empty boasts and idle threats. It was as if the past two years had never happened and he was in euphoric recall for the referendum campaign. The last time he had really felt the public's love. A time of fantasy when he could believe in miracles and they would come true.

Belief. That's what he demanded of those around him in the Conservative party. It wasn't that the prime minister's Lancaster House speech had run aground on the realities of Brexit. It was that she just hadn't believed enough in what she was doing. She had got lost 'in a fog of self doubt' and her Chequers white paper would submit the UK to the EU's 'vassalage' and leave us in a state of permanent limbo. All-too-familiar yadda. The therapy of mindless mindlessness.

Boris did not stop to explain why he had initially been only too happy to sign up to the Chequers deal and had only resigned after being shamed into doing so by David Davis. Then Boris isn't much given to introspection. Primarily because there's almost nothing to see. Strip away the vanity and the ego and there's a giant void. A black hole of misery that he's hellbent on inflicting on others.

For 12 minutes Boris bumbled on. Neither making a direct leadership challenge, nor pledging his support. Rubbishing the Chequers deal without giving any sign he had anything better to offer. Just bluster and lies. There were a few reassuring cheers and pats on the shoulder from his handful of friends when he finally limped to the end of his speech, but they were more of sympathy than acclaim. The send-off to an embarrassing relative you hope not to see again.

They had come in search of a saviour lion and found only a paper tiger. If Boris was the answer, they had long since forgotten what the question was. Maybe they really were better off with May after all. A thought that was as terrifying to them as it is to the rest of the country.

Enter Dominic Raab, a veritable chip off the old Brexit block

19 JULY 2018

There is no sincerer form of flattery. It had been expected that the appointment of Dominic Raab to replace David Davis as Brexit secretary might raise the average IQ of the department by a few dozen points. After all, even appointing my dog – one of the dimmer creatures on this planet – would have been an improvement. But these hopes have been quickly dashed. Either there is something about the Brexit department that renders all ministers who work for it catatonically stupid or Raab is determined to live down to the standards of his predecessor. An act of kindness.

What Raab does have, however, that Davis doesn't, is a limited amount of self-awareness. He realises that the whole purpose of his job is that it's entirely cosmetic. He's not there to actually do anything. He's there to give the impression that he's doing something. The Brexit negotiations are far too complex to be left to any of the halfwits in the Brexit department. They're also way too tricky for the prime minister and the civil service, but it's they who are calling the shots and Raab's main function is to do the photocopying and make the tea. Jobs he can just about manage.

At his first departmental questions, Raab immediately set about proving his lack of credentials by declaring he was very much looking forward to Michel Barnier offering 'his full support' for the Chequers white paper when they met later in the day. A curious reading of the situation, given that the other EU countries have been openly sniggering about the white paper's faults for much of the past few days and were under the impression they were currently still negotiating the withdrawal agreement. Raab hadn't got to where he had today by knowing what he was doing. Or what was going on. The ghost of Davis past.

The general sense of futility around Brexit is catching. When Hilary Benn first became chair of the Brexit select committee, his questions to ministers in the Commons came with bite. A sense of real anger that the government was failing in its duty to the country. Now they come with the weary resignation of a man who knows he is an eyewitness to an ongoing major pile-up but is powerless to prevent it. Would the minister care to talk through how he was going to avoid a hard border in Northern Ireland, Benn sighed, more in hope than expectation. Not really, Raab shrugged. It would be fine because it would be fine because it would be fine. That's about as far as anyone in government has really got. It was the same with the services sector. The reason no one had got

37

around to thinking about it was because it was only 80% of the economy so it wasn't that important.

The shadow Brexit secretary, Keir Starmer, felt obliged to try a couple of questions on the viability of the Chequers agreement but he, too, was sweet-talked with meaningless circular arguments that went nowhere. A world of magical realism where everything could be simultaneously exactly the same and entirely different. Here and not here. Where there would be a Brexit dividend even if the country was worse off because being worse off was a price worth paying for taking back control.

It wasn't just Labour that was getting fobbed off. Several of the hardcore Tory Eurosceptics were keen to make sure ministers were making detailed plans for their preferred no-deal Brexit. Absolutely, Raab insisted. The department had started thinking about it very hard a few days previously and had already come up with some nicely coloured wall charts he hoped would be made available to the public at some point in the future when it would all be a bit late. But it would still all be fine even if it wasn't.

At this point, Steve Baker, the former junior Brexit minister who had been Private Walker to Davis's Captain Mainwaring and is now a self-appointed cheerleader for Boris Johnson, intervened to ask if his one-page master-plan – MY MASTERPLAN by S. BAKER. 1. Tell the EU to sod off. 2. Take back control 3. So there. 4. Panic – could be widely distributed around the department. Are you sure? Raab said. Wouldn't it be less embarrassing if it was quietly fed through the shredder?

Baker wasn't satisfied. It's not enough for him to be thought an idiot. He won't rest until he's proved it. So he carried on, demanding also that the minister appoint a tame economist to rubbish the HMRC report that warned even a soft Brexit would cost the country jobs and money. Raab said nothing. It didn't feel the time to point out Brexit had already cost Baker his job and there was every chance it would claim those of several more ministers. The sooner the better. For their sake as well as the country's.

* * *

It was with some relief that parliament broke up for the summer recess at the end of July. For Theresa May it was welcome respite from the open dissent both within her cabinet and the Tory party as a whole. For everyone else it was a time to enjoy the heatwave that had gripped Britain. Not that the government's Brexit problems entirely eased up. On July 26th, Michel Barnier formally rejected the UK's proposal to collect customs duties on its behalf, while just three days later Ministers revealed plans to send in the army to deliver food, medicine and fuel supplies if Britain left the EU without a deal. It was also reported that supermarkets were beginning to stockpile supplies. Not exactly the positive message of reassurance that Brexit was entirely on track that most of the country wanted to hear.

Still, there was always Boris Johnson to act as a distraction from the government's shortcomings. Since leaving office as foreign secretary, Johnson had quickly resumed his £250k per year gig as the Daily Telegraph's star columnist – being in government had come at the price of much financial hardship – and in early August he provoked controversy by writing an article in which he said that Muslim women wearing burqas looked like 'letter boxes' and 'bank robbers'. Johnson merely shrugged it off. Much as he had always dismissed all his many previous offensive statements over the years. And as before, he appeared Teflon-coated, riding out the storm as right-wing friends in the media rallied to his defence. Yet again, Johnson had got away with something that might have ended the career of almost any other politician.

Towards the end of August, when it hoped no one was paying much attention, the government sneaked out the first in a series of papers on its plans for a no-deal Brexit. They did not make great reading. Import and export declarations would be needed on all goods going across the border and importers would have to learn how to classify their goods in relation to World Trade Organization tariffs.

Six weeks' worth of medicines would be stockpiled by the government and pharmaceutical companies were advised to do the same. Northern Irish companies doing *business with the Republic were told to ask Dublin for guidance. Businesses should expect higher transaction costs with other EU countries and UK exporters of organic food could expect a nine-month block to sales.*

Other than that, everything would be more or less fine. Apart from what might be revealed in subsequent government papers. Fingers crossed and all that. The next parliamentary session could be a bumpy ride.

Dominic Raab reduced to the lowest common denominator of stupidity

4 SEPTEMBER 2018

The Commons got back to business after the summer recess with a deadening sense of déjà vu. The House broke up in July with the Brexit secretary trying to convince himself as much as anyone else that the UK was genuinely getting somewhere in the EU negotiations, and it returned to find him doing much the same thing.

Dominic Raab was ostensibly in the House to give a statement updating MPs on the progress of his recent talks with Michel Barnier but, as there hadn't been any, he chose instead to ad lib. The break has been kind to the Brexit secretary. In July, he looked tense and sweaty and would get tetchy if anyone dared contradict him, but now he appeared more urbane and confident at the dispatch box.

Unfortunately for him, it was the confidence of a man who had forgotten just how sidelined and out of his depth he really was.

Everything was going really well, Raab declared breathlessly. Apart from the bits that were going extremely badly. The talks had been injected with a new pace and intensity – they now ate sandwiches at the negotiating table rather than taking a two-hour break for lunch – and agreement had been reached in some key areas. The EU and the UK had settled on who would do the photocopying (they would take it in turns) and only semi-skimmed milk would be used for the coffee.

There were still a few problems, mind. Northern Ireland was still proving a bit tricky but he was sure it would get resolved one way or another without war breaking out. There again, maybe not. On the bright side, a no-deal wouldn't be as bad as all that. We would be keeping a six-week stockpile of medicines, so there was a fair chance that no one would die unnecessarily immediately. And if everyone put aside a few cans of baked beans, then no one should starve while the government tried to come up with a better plan.

'There are some risks to a no-deal scenario,' Raab generously conceded. But, one way or another, the UK would be ready for Brexit next March. His voice rather tailed off as he added that last bit, as he realised the fundamental absurdity of what he was saying. The UK is going to be ready for nothing. The only Brexit we are going to get is

42

the one the government manages to smuggle past both the EU and parliament. And right now it doesn't have a clue what that might be.

Keir Starmer sighed. The shadow Brexit secretary had hoped that Raab might prove to be a bit brighter than the dim David Davis, but there was clearly something about the nature of the job that reduced every incumbent to the lowest common denominator of stupidity. Still, Starmer was willing to do his job even if Raab wasn't up to doing his, so he read out the same checklist of questions that he always asked on these occasions. Questions he knew weren't going to be answered.

Was Raab aware that time was running out to get a deal? In July he had said he would have the outline of a deal by October. Now he was suggesting it would come in November at the earliest. When was he going to get round to dealing with Northern Ireland? And was he aware that saying a no-deal wouldn't be the end of the world wasn't the most inspiring rhetoric?

The Brexit secretary bristled. He doesn't like having his obvious shortcomings pointed out so forensically. He was doing better than Labour would have, he snapped. Hard to refute, but equally hard to believe.

There was one upside for Raab. As everyone knows that it is now the prime minister who is calling the shots and the Brexit secretary has less authority than the Four Pot Plants, none of the big-name Tories such as Boris Johnson, Iain Duncan Smith, Jacob Rees-Mogg,

Ken Clarke and Anna Soubry bothered to turn up to give him a hard time. The worst of the friendly fire was the deranged Owen Paterson insisting that Northern Ireland could easily be sorted out with technology that hadn't been invented yet. Someone call a doctor.

So it was left to Labour's Hilary Benn, Yvette Cooper and Chuka Umunna to deliver a few home truths. The Chequers deal was dead in the water. Barnier said so. The Tory right said so. And Labour said so. So wouldn't the government be better off coming up with a new plan and working out what it was going to do if it couldn't get any deal through parliament.

'Ssssh,' whispered Raab. This was the kind of careless talk that could cost lives if the EU got wind of it. At this point some MPs began to wonder if Raab actually had been born yesterday.

One plus one equals a trillion in the Brexiters' theatre of the absurd

11 SEPTEMBER 2018

Shortly before 11am, committee room nine began to fill up. First in were Owen Paterson, Steve Baker, Peter Bone, David Davis, Iain Duncan Smith, Bill Cash and Andrew Bridgen. Next was Matt Ridley. Always useful to have a climate change denier who destroyed Northern Rock onboard. Then came Jacob Rees-Mogg, followed a short while later by a sleep-deprived Boris Johnson, trying to slip in unnoticed. A full house. Just about all those whom no sane person would dream of leaving in charge of the country were gathered together to tell the world how they proposed to run the country if given half a chance.

It was all very confusing. Last week, we were told by the Brexiters that they would be announcing their alternative cunning plan to the prime minister's Chequers deal this week, only for them to change their mind when it was revealed the best they could come up with was to turn the UK into a tax haven, spend billions on a 'star wars' defence system and invade the Argies.

Then, on Monday night, Duncan Smith insisted it wasn't the job of backbench MPs to come up with credible alternatives. Fortunately, that still left room for some entirely incredible alternatives. Though Rees-Mogg was careful to explain that this alternative plan wasn't necessarily the alternative plan.

The event had been billed as 'economists for free trade'. The plural turned out to be optimistic, as there was only one economist in the room. And only then if you apply the term 'economist' very loosely. Patrick Minford is a man who has made a career out of being wrong about nearly everything, and he wasn't about to break the habit of a lifetime.

Every other economist had predicted a no-deal Brexit would lead to a 7% decline per year in GDP over the next

15 years. But Minford had news for them: they had all been looking at their graphs the wrong way up. If you turned them all upside down then the UK would see an unprecedented 7% year-on-year increase in GDP. It was simple, if only you knew how. Far from being broke, we were going to have an extra £1.1 trillion to spend.

It rapidly got even better than that. If Brexit caused a devaluation of the pound then everyone would be a lot better off. But if Brexit pushed the pound higher then we would also all be a lot better off. There literally were no downsides to Brexit. Nothing could possibly go wrong because 'any competent government would sort out any problems'. Minford had rather missed yet another obvious flaw in his argument. Looking around the room, it was hard to spot anyone who would count as competent.

Johnson's eyes began to close – it's been a rough few days – and even Rees-Mogg, looking increasingly like an undertaker in an oversize suit, didn't appear entirely convinced by Minford's analysis. After thanking him for his work, he advised everyone not to be too concerned about the exact figures. Rather to just concentrate on the fact that everything was going to be great if we left with a no-deal Brexit. So great that he now said his preferred option was something entirely different to what Minford had proposed. What he really wanted was a Canada-style deal. Just because he wanted to be friendly with the EU. Apparently.

Things really began to fall apart, though, when the media were invited to ask questions. Though Rees-Mogg tried to keep order, several of the Tory MPs were less than impressed – Duncan Smith and Cash were especially grumpy – that no one seemed to be taking any of their ideas in the slightest bit seriously and were only interested in whether this was an open challenge to Theresa May and, if so, whether Johnson was leading it.

'This isn't about personalities,' snapped Baker. Johnson looked surprised at that. Why else was he hanging out with these people he didn't really like if not to get their support for his ambition? He had meant to try to get through the hour without saying anything, but then his narcissism got the better of him. He tried to find some words, but only managed to mumble something incoherent that brought him sympathetic applause from his embarrassed colleagues, who were beginning to look as desperate as he was.

There was just time for one more spat, as Baker insisted he was a numbers man and he had all the numbers he needed – one plus one equals one trillion – before a relieved Rees-Mogg drew the event to a close. Johnson left the room and promptly headed the wrong way down a dead end. It had been that sort of day. A theatre of the absurd.

* * *

After a fortnight back in action, the Commons took a three-week break for the conference season. That time of the year when every party briefly forgets about taking on its opponents and concentrates on fighting among itself.

As usual it was the Lib Dems who went first. Ever since the party had been all but wiped out at the 2015 general election, the Lib Dem conference had tended to resemble a rather depressing end-of-the-pier show. One that knew its time was up, but couldn't bring itself to admit it in public. Despite the leader, Vince Cable, doing his best to put a damper on proceedings by failing to say when exactly he would be stepping down – he hadn't exactly energised the party – this year's conference did have more of a spring in its step.

Six months previously, no one had given the calls for a people's vote – aka a second referendum – more than a passing thought. Now it was beginning to gain serious traction. This may have been as much down to the hopelessness of the government's negotiating tactics as the demands from Remainers, but the Lib Dems weren't about to look a gift horse in the mouth. A glimmer of hope was on the horizon.

Meanwhile, Theresa May had other problems. Before her own party conference, she was due to go to an informal summit in Salzburg where she was due to hear the EU verdict on her Brexit plans. It was worse than even she expected.

Theresa May in denial after her Salzburg ordeal

20 SEPTEMBER 2018

If it hadn't all been so numbingly inevitable, it might have been possible to feel sorry for Theresa May. Back in the UK, both Remainers and Leavers had pronounced her Chequers' proposals to be dead in the water, but the prime minister had still travelled to the informal EU summit in Salzburg hoping for a stay of execution. A few lukewarm words and some insincere air kisses at the very least, until after she had survived the Conservative party conference. Her current range of vision really is that limited.

Instead she got a lesson in plain-speaking brutality. No attempts to sugar the pill, as EU leader after leader took it in turns to dismiss Chequers and to mock the UK over its lack of progress in its Brexit preparations. Even the Dutch thought they were better prepared for a no-deal Brexit than us. It was left to Donald Tusk, president of the EU Council, to deliver the coup de grâce. The Chequers deal was unworkable because it undermined the integrity of the single market. And, by the way, its solution to the Northern Ireland border was just fantasy.

Moments after being given the bad news in person, May had to face the UK media. The room in which the press conference was held was small and airless, but the prime minister was already sweaty when she walked in.

More than that, she looked angry and terrified. Alone and out of her depth, her eyes darting across the room, searching for one friendly face. There wasn't one. There hadn't been one in the two days she had been in Austria.

May did what she always does when she's up against it. She went into denial. Stick her fingers in her ears and pretend absolutely nothing had happened. Nothing had changed. She began by highlighting the important work on people trafficking and national security that had been discussed before – almost as an afterthought – getting round to Brexit. Ah yes, Brexit. 'Our white paper remains the only serious, credible proposal,' she said nervily. 'And I am confident we shall reach a deal.' Nothing really had changed. Madness.

There were a few seconds of silence as everyone took this in. It almost felt intrusive to observe the prime minister visibly falling apart. A public humiliation on the epic scale of both her refusal to accept the reversal of the dementia tax during the general election campaign and her car-crash leader's speech at last year's Tory party conference. Then May composed herself as best she could and invited the kicking she knew was coming her way. Bring it on. Everyone else had had a go so she might as well let the media have theirs. The martyrdom of St Theresa.

Her head swivelled back and forth frantically several times as she tried to pick out Laura Kuenssberg. She just couldn't get her eyes to focus. Eventually, May spotted the BBC's political editor, sitting where she had been all along, in the front row just a couple of feet from where she was standing. As the inevitable questions came, challenging her version of reality, the prime minister couldn't help but disconnect and go full Maybot. She wasn't there, no one was there. All she had to do was to hang on for the next 10 minutes and the ordeal would be over.

'I'm negotiating hard to give the British people what they voted for,' she said mindlessly, playing for time. Except she wasn't. Almost no one had voted for the level of helplessness that was all she apparently had to offer. If the EU did have concerns, she continued, reluctantly admitting that – just possibly – there were objections to her Chequers plan, then she wanted to sit down and hear them. The last 24 hours were now a total blank. She had completely forgotten she had spent them sitting down listening to the EU's concerns.

The digging became ever more fevered as her facial expressions became more contorted. Too much more of this and she would have become a dead ringer for Munch's *The Scream*. She did have a counterproposal but everyone would have to wait until she had thought of what it was. In any case, the EU were really just kidding – they did like to have their little European jokes – and would come round and see sense in the end. Just wait and see.

As quickly as decently possible, May made her excuses and left, keeping her head down, fearful that she might burst into tears if she made eye contact with anyone. If the shame didn't get her, then the pity would. She had been laid bare. The naked prime minister. Sans eyes, sans teeth, sans everything.

Theresa May excels herself in another exercise in futility

21 SEPTEMBER 2018

Was this the moment Theresa May finally lost all touch with reality? The day the Maybot's circuits overloaded and reverted to their factory settings. The day when history was rewritten in such a way as to make it virtually unrecognisable.

Shortly after midday rumours started to circulate that the prime minister was going to make a statement at 1.45pm. An important one. A lectern and flags job. The sense of panic was palpable. And not just inside No 10. Everyone felt it. The combination of the prime minister, a lectern and an unscheduled statement usually signifies turmoil for the country and disaster for her. A general election? A resignation? A visitation from Bono? Anything was possible.

As it happened we nearly didn't get any statement at all. The power had gone down inside No 10 and there was no live news feed. Sometimes the metaphors write themselves. But when she did eventually appear, 20 minutes later than planned, we were treated to the bizarre sight of May barricading herself inside No 10 with a solitary BBC cameraman – she clearly didn't trust either the lectern not to blow over in the wind or the assembled hacks outside not to ask awkward questions at the end – to announce that what she had said on Thursday in her press conference (which went disastrously and ended in humiliation) was what she had actually meant to say all along.

May, who has turned exercises in futility into an artform during her time in office, excelled herself this time. Nothing had changed from yesterday, when nothing had changed from the day before. Except this time she wanted to appear determined and steely instead of sweaty and terrified. She had looked into the abyss of her own career and decided that if she was going down then she would do her best to take her party and the country with her.

The Salzburg summit hadn't gone very well, she began. Nothing like a statement of the obvious to get things rolling. But now she wanted to make some things very clear to the EU. Cue her best death stare. The one she usually reserves for Boris Johnson. What she was clear about was that the Chequers plan – rubbished by many Tories, dismissed by the EU leaders and without a prayer of getting through parliament – was still the plan she intended to get through parliament and get the EU to accept.

As a denial of reality it was already a bravura performance, but within minutes things had lurched into another space-time continuum. One that even Stephen Hawking could never have imagined. Everything was basically the EU's fault. It was the EU that had forced the UK into leaving the EU. It was the EU that was making the UK confront the possibility of a hard Irish border because the UK had voted to leave. She had fallen over backwards to come up with a sensible solution and the EU had come up with none of their own. Other than, of course, to make it clear right from the start that the Canada and Norway models were the only options available and there could be no cherrypicking. Madness.

'I've never treated the EU with anything other than respect,' she said, her bottom lip quivering with what she hoped was righteous indignation. And she wanted some respect back. She had a point. She could have handled things better – face it, almost anyone could – but the EU could also have been slightly less charmless. But then they were probably only following the example of Boris and the other Brexiters who make a point of disrespecting May on an almost daily basis. Maybe Donald Tusk and Emmanuel Macron had got the impression she liked being treated that way.

May appears now as a woman with almost no respect for herself. Otherwise she would have long since walked away from a job she clearly does not like and a Brexit in which she does not believe. She knows she is compromised and she hates herself for it. It shows in every gurn, in every awkward hand gesture.

54

With a quick 180-degree turn, she left the room. A statement that had been meant to make her appear resolute had only highlighted her weakness. An exercise in damage limitation – to wash away the sins of Salzburg – that had always been doomed to failure. When you don't have anything to say, it's usually best to say nothing. But May just couldn't stop herself from carrying on digging.

Hard Brexiters' new plan gets A+ for idiocy

24 SEPTEMBER 2018

Take two. A fortnight ago, Jacob Rees-Mogg, David Davis, Steve Baker, Boris Johnson and other leading members of the European Research Group squeezed themselves into a Westminster committee room to share their excitement at having found a single economist who was optimistic about Brexit. Here was the way forward. Ignore the doom-mongers, just crash out of the EU on World Trade Organization terms and the UK would be more than £1 trillion better off. Happy days all round.

Until today, when many of the usual suspects – with the exception of Boris, who tweeted his undying solidarity with anything and anyone that helped him become Tory leader – rattled around in a barely half full Gladstone library of the Liberal Club to tell a handful of reporters that – much to their surprise – they had found a second economist who was tremendously enthusiastic about Brexit. Only he had come up with a completely different model – something more akin to a Canada-style trade deal – so that's what they were now endorsing. Fickle doesn't begin to describe them. Though simple-minded might.

Shanker Singham, the author of the IEA's 'Plan A+', was introduced as the country's leading trade lawyer. Which rather suggested there can't be much competition for that coveted title, as Singham immediately did his best to live down to expectations. The problem with the Brexit negotiations so far, he declared confidently, was that we had been treating them as a problem singular to the UK and the EU. Silly, silly us. His reasoning was all to be found in footnote 28 on page 37 of his report. Which didn't appear to exist.

What we should have been doing is signing loads of other trade deals with the US and the rest of the world behind the EU's back – the US was apparently just gagging to do deals before it knew what final trade arrangement we had agreed with the EU – because the EU would definitely never have found out was going on and pointed out its illegality, said the country's leading trade lawyer, failing to grasp the basics of international trade.

As if to prove he really was as stupid as he sounded, Singham went on to suggest that post-Brexit, the UK might do some individual trade deals with separate EU countries. He concluded by saying that deregulation was the way forward – British workers deserved the same rights to be crushed to death by collapsing buildings as their counterparts in Bangladesh – and that Brexit could make the whole world about 10% richer. After several decades in which everyone was at least 10% poorer.

The four politicians on the panel heroically maintained the idiocy quotient. The former Labour MP Gisela Stuart excelled herself by claiming that Brexit was actually a game of four-dimensional chess and we needed negotiators who could rise above the two-dimensional. Which rather ruled out everyone on the panel as you wouldn't trust any of them not to lose a game of draughts to a five-year-old.

Rees-Mogg loftily declared that he had already solved the problem of the Irish border in a previous presentation, that had been dismissed out of hand as fantasy by everyone who understands the issues, and so there was no reason why Theresa May shouldn't immediately accept these new proposals as government policy. Other than the fact that even she recognised them to be unworkable. Which is saying something.

The last word went to David Davis, who can seldom resist the opportunity of saying something he will later regret. Most deals were really only finalised in the last 48 seconds, he insisted. Which explained both why he had invariably come off worse in all negotiations and why he had done almost nothing during his time as Brexit secretary. The possibility now has to be entertained that Davis has been an undercover agent for staying in the EU all along. It's the only rational explanation.

If there is a third economist who thinks Brexit is going to benefit the UK, she wasn't to be found in Liverpool, where the Labour party was going through massive contortions at its conference to find a way of keeping everyone happy. And pleasing no one. While everyone seemingly agreed Brexit was a terrible idea. The party leadership seemed to think the solution lay in only offering people a vote on a bad deal or an even worse deal. Clowns to the left, jokers to the right.

Labour's Brexit plan: to have an illusion of a plan, not an actual plan

25 SEPTEMBER 2018

Confused? You soon will be. After an hour in which delegates argued about constitutional arrangements and conference procedures which only they appeared to fully understand, Keir Starmer was finally called to the lectern to begin the Brexit debate. It was a question of priorities. First things first.

'Just when we need a strong government, what do we see?' he began. 'Division. Chaos.' You had to admire his honesty. Trying to keep up with Labour's internal manoeuvrings on its Brexit proposals over the previous 24 hours had proved to be next to impossible.

Despite having come up with a composite motion that

was sufficiently vaguely worded to mean whatever anyone wanted it to mean, the shadow chancellor, John McDonnell, had already managed to disagree with himself in two separate interviews on just what a people's vote would signify.

At this rate, Labour will soon need to give hourly updates on its latest policy positions. Assuming anyone knows.

Having apologised for his own party's failings, the shadow Brexit secretary turned his attention to the Tories. They were at war over Chequers, had no credible plan and Labour would vote down any deal that involved a bad, vague or blind Brexit. So far, so on message. Nothing that anyone didn't already know – even Barry Gardiner, never the sharpest member of the shadow cabinet, who, at a fringe event, hadn't appeared to know Labour was meant to be talking up the possibility of a general election. Though it was just possible he was ahead of the policy curve rather than behind it.

As he neared the end of his speech Starmer glanced to his left and noticed that Jeremy Corbyn wasn't in the hall. Out of sight, out of mind, so he decided to veer off from his agreed text and ad lib. When it came to a people's vote, no one would be ruling out Remain as an option. There were a few astonished gasps and then at least half of a near full auditorium rose to give him a standing ovation. This is what they had come to the conference for. To be offered some hope on Brexit. And their faith had been rewarded.

Starmer appeared genuinely surprised by the reaction. His delivery has always tended towards the forensic rather than the motivational, and his speeches are normally rewarded with polite rather than appreciative applause. He blushed a little and let the love wash over him. He could get used to this. Labour policy had been rewritten yet again, live in the conference hall.

Not everyone was quite so delighted though. The Labour MP Dennis Skinner and several hundred others remained motionless in their seats, their faces locked in a furious rictus disbelief. This wasn't just a betrayal of a vital Labour party principle that anything contentious be debated in private, it was a betrayal of all Labour supporters who had voted Leave in the referendum campaign. The result was sacrosanct and it was just too bad if things didn't turn out to be quite so rosy as had been promised.

With just 90 minutes allocated to Brexit – it wasn't as if it was a matter of national existential crisis – several delegates chose to use their turn on the platform as group therapy.

Tim Roache, of the GMB union, vented his hatred of Blairites – always good to keep the real enemy in your sights – while Aslef's Tosh McDonald rolled back the years to share three decades of unresolved pain. He had hated Margaret Thatcher so much, he confessed, that he used to set his alarm clock an hour early so he could get an extra 60 minutes of hate into his day. The crowd let out a primal scream of recognition.

It took Unite's Steve Turner to refocus the conference on Brexit. Starmer had been out of order, he said. And would be taken out and shot in the dog exercise area within the hour. If there was a people's vote – not that there would be if he had anything to do with it – the simple choice would be giving everyone the chance to decide on whether they wanted to have two arms sawn off or just the one. It was unthinkable that anyone might be given the option of keeping both arms. That would be against the will of the people. And against the will of the Labour party, whose newly revised official Brexit policy was to have an illusion of a plan rather than an actual plan.

Brexit had been reduced to a game of cards that neither the Tories nor Labour actually knew how to win. Leaving both sides circling one another, hoping the other blinked first and made the fatal mistake. This could get bloody.

Boris does his best Boris tribute act for Tory conference

2 OCTOBER 2018

Say what you like about Boris Johnson, he delivers a second-rate speech better than most other second-rate politicians, many of whom have been on show at the Tory party conference in Birmingham this week. But the bottom line is that Boris is essentially still second rate. A man who imagines himself to be a latter-day Winston Churchill, but is nothing more than an ersatz Donald

61

Trump with little to offer other than his own narcissism masquerading as cheap populism.

Yet in the land of the blind, the one-eyed man is king, and Johnson is what passes for stardust in the Brexit circles of the Tory party. A faint flicker, raging against the dying of the light, as he struggles to avoid being sucked into the black hole. And for his one scheduled appearance at a fringe event, hundreds of delegates were queueing outside the 1,500-seater hall some two hours before he was due on stage. This was the golden ticket. A message of hope for the hopeless.

Shortly before the start, the usual VIP suspects began to fill the front row. David Davis, Steve Baker, Priti Patel, Owen Paterson, Andrea Jenkyns, John Redwood and Andrew Bridgen. The same crew that had been at almost every 'Chuck Chequers' event. None of whom most sane people would trust anywhere near government. The scene was set. This wasn't going to be a serious speech so much as an act of communion for the already converted. A greatest hits rally at which Boris would deliver his own Boris tribute act.

Johnson bumbled on to stage. Bumbling was what people expected of him – his trademark trope – and he didn't want to disappoint. The audience rose to give him their first standing ovation and he relaxed a little. He still had the magic. 'It's great bumble bumble to be bumble bumble in Birmingham bumble bumble,' he bumbled, before insisting that he was standing before everyone 'with all humility'. Always good to get the first lie in early. Boris has never done humble in his life.

After that he was straight on to autopilot. A lot more bumble bumbling, a bit of hair tugging and the occasional thump of the lectern to suggest he actually cared about what he was saying. Pretty much the same speech he had given the time before and the time before that. The same feeble gags about Toblerones and bus shelters that never failed to get a few desultory laughs from people starved of genuine humour. The same sob story about how he had once felt sorry for a couple in a Wolverhampton council house. The same lies about things the EU had never done and what the Labour party planned to do. Always the lies.

Bumble bumble. Loud whoops from the audience. Bumble bumble. The same broken record of why Boris thought that Boris would make a great prime minister and couldn't believe that the whole world didn't agree with Boris. He ran through a totally uncosted housing programme; he did a drive-by shooting of Michael Gove; he boasted of his record as foreign secretary. That last bit didn't take long.

Then Boris turned his attention to Theresa May and Brexit. Chequers was against the law – it wasn't, but what the hell? – and Britain was being cheated. What was needed was someone like Boris who would bumble bumble, make Latin references, ruffle his hair and say that Britain could be great again if only we believed enough. Someone who lacked even the basic level of self-awareness to realise he had broken the system and had no real idea how to fix it. Someone whose only visible plan was to say sod off to the EU and that if it was very lucky we would let it trade with us again sometime in the future.

Same old, same old. A vision of the future in which Boris was prime minister and the country was condemned to a seventh circle of hell in which the same speech, the same jokes, the same Latin would be played on a loop indefinitely. Then a rare moment of clarity. Pathos even. Boris looked down at the front row and saw just a handful of the same hopeful faces. He might have the numbers to stop Chequers, but he was way short of what he would need to become prime minister. His speech bumble bumble tailed off into silence. As so often, he had made a splash. But the waters would soon close over.

Too long and devoid of content, May's speech is a total success

3 OCTOBER 2018

Look on the bright side. No one gave the prime minister a P45. Her voice just about held out. And the video screen backdrop with the word 'opportunity' on it didn't develop a glitch and switch to 'porn' instead. After avoiding all that, anything else would be near enough an unqualified success.

Not that there weren't a few awkward moments in the buildup. As members of the cabinet trooped in to the hall, it became clear there weren't enough seats for David Lidington, Sajid Javid, Jeremy Hunt and Philip Hammond. Either they are not wanted on voyage or someone in the government can't count. Four ordinary punters were unceremoniously hoiked out of the auditorium.

Then the attorney general, Geoffrey Cox, chose to use his 10-minute introduction as a pantomime audition. Blackadder channels Brian Blessed. The audience went wild and if the Tory party conference had ended at that point everyone would have gone home delirious. If there is a next year, Theresa May will be more careful in her choice of warm-up act. No one wants to be upstaged on their big day out.

Still, at least the prime minister nailed her entrance. As Abba's 'Dancing Queen' was played through the PA system, Theresa hoofed her way on stage doing a reprise of her cringe-inducing South African Peter Crouch dance. Whatever else she has achieved in her time in office, no one can say she hasn't worked hard at refining her Maybot image. This latest iteration looked the real deal. Britain: not just world leaders in AI, but a world leader as AI.

Having won over the hall with a little self depreca-tion, May reverted to the more familiar territory of living down to expectations. There was no way of getting away from it: though this was one of the best speeches she had made as prime minister it was still a Theresa May speech. As such, it was riddled with contradictions, largely devoid of content and went on at least a quarter of an hour too long as the algorithms buffered in a spinning circle of death.

'I want a party not for the few, not even for the many but for everyone who is willing to work hard and do their best,' she said. An almost perfect description of herself. No one can accuse May of not working hard or trying to do her best. It's just that these qualities aren't always quite enough in a prime minister who has turned mediocrity into an art form. What she wanted was a party where she could feel at home: whether her party actually wanted her as its leader was rather more in doubt. Many of the people who were politely applauding her had been cheering and whooping for Boris Johnson the day before.

Oblivious to the pathos, May ploughed on with a plea for national unity. Seemingly unaware of the irreconcilable splits in her own party, she made the case for the Tories being the party of inclusion. 'If your dad arrived on a plane from Pakistan, you can become home secretary,' she said. Yes. And once the government's proposed immigration plans come into force, your dad will be on the first plane back to Pakistan.

In a final, desperate, plea for someone, anyone, to love her, she begged a few Labour centrists to come and join her for a night in staring at the wall and sharing awkward silences.

Then she moved on to Brexit. Here she had a genuine announcement. She had listened to the party and was going to 'chuck Chequers'. As in 'chuck the name Chequers'. She was still going to press ahead with the Brexit deal that the EU, Labour and dozens of MPs in her own party had already said was unworkable. She just wasn't going to refer to it as Chequers any more. Instead it was going to be called 'Nothing at All'. Mainly because nothing at all had so far been agreed on Northern Ireland or the future trading relationship with the EU. But once nothing at all had been agreed she was absolutely clear that austerity was going to end and we would all have lots of money even if nothing at all was agreed. No wonder everyone looked a bit confused.

'Our best years lie ahead,' May declared. Thereby inadvertently drawing attention to the fact that everything had been – and still was – irredeemably awful for the past 10 years. But as a reward we would get to enjoy a Festival of Brexit Britain in 2022. To celebrate years of rationing and the fact that not all of us had died. Lucky, lucky us. Can't wait.

As the speech neared the hour mark, most people in the hall got a bit twitchy. You can have too much of an average thing. When May finally wound to a close, the audience clapped enthusiastically. Though not too enthusiastically. This was how the Tory conference ended. Not with a bang. Not even with a whimper. But with a stampede for the exits.

Theresa May puts her faith in the miracle of Schrödinger's Brexit

18 OCTOBER 2018

'You know what? I've had it up to here. I'm sick to death of going round in circles, trying to achieve the impossible. Brexit is a complete shitshow. You know it, I know it, everyone knows it. There is just no way any of this ends well, either for the country or for me.

'So let's stop pretending there's any way of making everyone happy. It's a car crash. Pure and simple. And if anyone thinks they can do better, then let them have a go. I'm done with being trolled by all and sundry. It was bad enough being humiliated on a daily basis by Boris Johnson, David Davis, Michel Barnier and Donald Tusk, but now even the Lithuanian prime minister is joining in. Enough's enough. So that's it. I'm out of here. Sayonara losers.'

That's the press conference Theresa May would like to have given at the end of yet another European Council meeting at which no progress had been made towards resolving the Northern Ireland border. Or anything else for that matter. Stalemate with the clock ticking. Sure, Tusk and Juncker hadn't actively trashed her as they had last time, but their efforts to sound reassuring had hardly been . . . reassuring. A bit like a surgeon coming in to see you just after surgery and saying: 'You'll be up and about in next to no time' when you've just had both your legs amputated.

Instead the prime minister inched her way slowly to the lectern. And breathe. This time she wasn't going to lose it, as she had in Salzburg. No wild staring or heavy sweating. She was going to zen this one out. She would go into shutdown, pretend she wasn't really there. Just say words, any words to get her out the other side. Set the mind to blank, survive the 15 minutes of pain and then she'd be on the next plane home.

There had been good progress on Brexit, she began. That was progress as in not actively going backwards. Or forwards. Given time, she was confident that a miracle might appear. That was it. All she had to say. Thank you and good night.

Journalists weren't quite so easily palmed off, and soon May was facing incoming from all directions. It was pointed out that she kept making all sorts of contradictory promises that she couldn't possibly keep. So when would she get off the fence and say who she was going to disappoint? May paused and went into automatic lockdown. That question hadn't existed so she was going to answer another one entirely. She was going to get a good deal that would deliver on the result of the referendum. The end.

Next she even surprised herself by channeling her hitherto unknown inner Marxist with a dialectic analysis. Things going so disastrously badly right now was actually a sign we were tantalisingly close to a deal. The time to worry was when the negotiations appeared to be running smoothly. A few blank looks appeared on the faces of the assembled hacks, but none as blank as the prime minister's. No one was better than her at being absent from her own life.

One by one her circuits shut down, so all that was left was a meaningless collection of random words plucked somewhere from deep inside her unconscious. When she had previously said she was open to the idea of an extension to the transition period she had in no way meant to give the impression she was open to the idea of an extension. Schrödinger's Brexit was back on again. The once and future extension that both did and didn't exist.

And with that she melted away. There had been no fine words. Not even a hint of defiance. A stronger leader, make that any sort of leader, might have observed that both Johnson and Davis had had their chance in government and achieved nothing of any note, so now was the time for her to impose her vision of the least damaging Brexit. But she couldn't even manage that. She had been running on empty for over a year. All May had to offer was her own sense of resignation. A life of quiet desperation. A life that was getting steadily quieter and more desperate by the day.

* * *

After months – years even – of negotiation, Theresa May was at last ready to announce her final Brexit deal that had been agreed with the EU. Members of the cabinet were summoned to No 10 to read the key documents to make sure they could agree to them. The central detail was the Northern Ireland backstop, for which the UK had agreed a joint arbitration panel with the EU to determine when it could be terminated. Hardline Brexiteers of the European Research Group immediately condemned the deal, saying they would vote against it. Boris Johnson declared it made the UK a vassal state.

PM finally unites party with Brexit deal that no one likes

13 NOVEMBER 2018

Theresa May – the prime minister with the unerring knack of snatching defeat from the jaws of defeat. Shortly after four in the afternoon, a tweet from the Irish broadcaster RTÉ, reporting that the UK and the EU had agreed an outline Brexit deal, sent Westminster hacks into meltdown. It also seemed to catch the government by surprise. Hard to believe, but May gave every appearance of being one of the last to know that she had secured a deal.

A competent prime minister might have used the time to press home her advantage. To give a television

71

statement in which she talked up the historic nature of her achievement. That she secured a Brexit deal that would deliver on the will of the people. The sunlit uplands were in touching distance. But May just couldn't bring herself to do that.

In her heart of hearts, she knew that her deal was a terrible deal. The only thing it had going for it was that it was better than no deal at all. Most of the promises she had made were now dust. She had achieved something most had thought impossible: she had come up with a deal that would be rejected by Remainers and Leavers alike. Faced with a personal humiliation, she rolled into a foetal ball and watched cartoons.

A short while later, one of her aides switched off the TV and told her it might be a good idea to try and get her cabinet on board. Once they had got over the surprise of her actually making a decision, one or two might have a few things to say about it. One of the first invited in was Chris Grayling. That's because he was a slow reader and it would take him a while to get his head round it. Give him a month or two and he might know whether he could support the deal or not. It was going to be a long night in Downing Street.

Over in the House of Commons, the hardline Brexit-ers of the European Research Group and the DUP could hardly believe their luck. TV abhors a vacuum. With no one from the government out and about to sell the deal, the airwaves were all theirs. Even though, like everyone else, they didn't have a clue what was actually in the deal, they were free to shitbag the one they thought she had probably got. And if it turned out they got the whole thing wrong, then no harm done. It was always therapeutic to let off steam and lay down some markers.

Boris Johnson was first into central lobby. Brexit had been betrayed. We were being to all intents and purposes kept in the customs union and the UK would remain in vassalage. Boom, bumble, boom, bumble, thank you and good night. Next up was Jacob Rees-Mogg. He too had no idea what the actual deal was. He was just certain that it was a bad one, because any deal that the EU signed off had to be bad for the UK.

Several other Tories milled around hopefully, desperate for someone to ask them for their views. Priti Patel and Mark Francois eventually sloped off, their voices largely unheard, their no-mark status confirmed. Iain Duncan Smith looked ecstatic. Almost as if he was far more thrilled the prime minister had got a deal he disliked rather than one he wanted. That way he could be properly, righteously, smugly outraged. Even if the cabinet backed May, then the party wouldn't and the government would fall, he predicted. When might it fall, he was asked. 'I'm not in the business of making predictions,' he snapped.

The DUP's Nigel Dodds was also in seventh heaven. A man never happier than when he is angry. He began by asking if anyone knew what the deal was. Everyone shrugged. Never mind, he continued, let's just proceed on the basis it's one that the DUP could not accept. Betrayal. Surrender. He continued in this vein till the last TV crew had left.

There was just one smiling face in the cabinet. Earlier in the day, David Lidington, the de facto deputy prime minister, had drawn the short straw as the public face of the government's climbdown on revealing the final legal advice on the Brexit deal. It had been a couple of hours in the chamber he would rather forget. And now he could. Along with everyone else. No one would remember his painful two hours of humble pie. All eyes were back on Theresa. Every cloud and all that . . .

* * *

Despite having played a central role in negotiating the UK's Brexit deal with the EU, Dominic Raab resigned as Brexit secretary two days later on 15 November claiming he was now unable to support the deal. Not taking responsibility for one's own actions was proving to be a common denominator of the May government. Raab, a hard Brexiteer, had been in office for just over four months. A day later, Theresa May appointed Stephen Barclay as his replacement. Barclay was given the job on the strict instructions that his prime role was to be entirely cosmetic. He would be allowed to do some general admin-istrative work – typing and that sort of thing – but on no account must he show any signs of doing any thinking for himself. Barclay was only too happy to oblige.

Dadaist PM and vague Corbyn make nonsense of current state of Brexit

18 NOVEMBER 2018

The drugs still aren't working. Or if they are, then Theresa May and Jeremy Corbyn have been given the wrong prescriptions. Both party leaders appeared on Sky's *Sophy Ridge on Sunday* politics show to make sense of the current state of the Brexit negotiations, and both departed with their credibility further diminished. Far from each having a vision for the future, they looked as if they would be lucky to find a way out of the building. Even with the exit signs clearly marked.

After an interview in Saturday's *Daily Mail* in which the prime minister tried to emphasise her human qualities – she might even have opened a can of baked beans last week! Who knew? – she was now back to her familiar stubborn, automaton self. No one was going to take her alive. If her own party wanted to come for her then let them bring it on. This was a fight to the death.

May began by arguing that her Brexit deal wasn't about her – a message that doesn't appear to have got through to her cabinet, her MPs or the rest of the country.

It was about the national interest. It was about getting a deal that was worse than what we already had and nothing like the one that had originally been promised. A deal against which everyone could unite. Ridge looked understandably confused but tried to pin her down.

Maybe they could start with something easy. What bit of the deal did she actually believe in? None of it, May replied confidently. Because it was in the national interest for her not to believe in it. Obviously the 570 pages of the withdrawal agreement weren't that great for the UK, but people shouldn't get too fixated on the details of the backstop agreements, because there was a vanishingly small possibility that they would never be put in place. Ridge sighed. Mainly with pleasure. This was TV gold. Getting the prime minister to say something stupid live on air is every interviewer's dream.

Chancing her arm, Ridge suggested there was a problem with the UK not being able to end the backstop unilaterally. May happily obliged with more spontaneous dadaism. It was like this. The backstop was like an insurance policy and no policy could be ended unilaterally. Here we had a prime minister all but admitting she needed permission to cancel her house insurance. And yes, she was furious at having to continue paying for policies she no longer needed. Like the home contents insurance at No 10.

In any case, people shouldn't get too fixated about the withdrawal agreement as that was all signed off

– something she had either omitted to tell Andrea Leadsom or that Leadsom was too stupid to have grasped – and concentrate on the future trade agreement. All seven pages of it. In the next week – she couldn't say exactly when as she hadn't checked availability on Eurostar – she was going back to Brussels in the hope of fleshing out the future trade agreement to another couple of pages of waffle. Nothing was agreed until everything was agreed. Ridge begged to differ. Everyone agreed she had won the interview hands down.

As she had with Corbyn earlier in the programme. The Labour leader didn't get off to the best of starts, admitting he hadn't read the entire withdrawal agreement. Obviously almost no one else in parliament has done so either – and those that have, apart from a few lawyers who make a living from disagreeing on its meaning, have failed to understand its full meaning – but it wasn't a great look for someone who wants to be prime minister.

Corbyn did manage to clarify how Labour couldn't stop Brexit on its own, but was at a loss when asked to square how Labour could negotiate a deal as good as the one the UK already had with the EU when the EU had categorically stated it was a non-starter.

But it was on the second referendum that he really struggled. It wasn't something for now, but for the future. Except with just 131 days till 29 March, the future is pretty much now and Corbyn appeared to have no views on what choices should be on a second referendum or how he would vote if there was one. Rather he was going to pin all his hopes on voting down May's deal and a no-deal and cross his fingers that the government would call a general election even though it definitely wouldn't. Shares in Ridge soared, just as shares in the UK plunged.

Still, May and Corbyn were visions of clarity compared with Dominic Raab over on *The Andrew Marr Show*. The former Brexit secretary imagines himself to be a natural leader, a Marvel superhero. The rest of the world sees him as Captain Mainwaring in Lycra. A genuinely comic comic-book hero.

He had resigned as Brexit secretary because his support for the prime minister was so firm and unwavering that it was better expressed from the backbenches. The withdrawal agreement he had helped to negotiate was nothing like the deal he had helped to negotiate. People dying as a result of a no-deal Brexit was no biggie because they could have been run over and killed on a B road. Cometh the hour, cometh the man. Bizarrely, a few people other than Raab appear to believe he could be that man. Time for the hard hats.

* * *

Throughout the autumn, the hardline Tory Brexiteers of the European Research Group had threatened to trigger a vote of no confidence in the prime minister by submitting letters to Graham Brady, the chair of the 1922 backbench committee. There would be weekly rumours of just who had or hadn't submitted their letters. The number of letters required to force a no confidence vote was 48, but Brady was the model of discretion in not disclosing how many letters he had received – or indeed had been submitted and subsequently withdrawn. As a result no one ever knew exactly how close to that number the ERG actually was. As chairman of the ERG, Jacob Rees-Mogg had hoped that the submission of his no confidence letter would prove the symbolic tipping point. As it happened, it turned out that some of his ERG colleagues may not have been telling the truth about having written their own letters.

How many letters are there in ERG? Not 48, that's for sure

20 NOVEMBER 2018

Would you believe it? The European Research Group had significantly overestimated the number of people attending the launch of its new paper – why the UK should tell the EU to sod off: part 183 – and there were a few dozen empty seats by the time the event got under way at a converted church in Westminster. Perhaps a few of the invitation letters had gone astray. Or some of those who promised to attend just hadn't shown up.

At a previous ERG event to launch an earlier paper – why the UK should tell the EU to sod off: part 156 – the Conservative MP Steve Baker declared himself to be a 'numbers man'. As in, making up the numbers. In both senses. Ever since the former junior Brexit secretary was promoted to well above his pay grade as Jacob Rees-Mogg's second-in-command, the ERG has struggled with basic maths.

For several months, the group had claimed it was only one or two letters short of the 48 needed to trigger a vote of confidence in the prime minister. So when Rees-Mogg announced that he too had sent his letter to the chairman of the 1922 Committee, Baker quickly predicted the 48 threshold would be reached within a day or so. However, it's turned out there have been far fewer letters sent than had been promised. More imaginary numbers.

Quite what has happened to the other letters is unexplained. Given that many members of the ERG aren't the brightest, it's possible that some Tory MPs either forgot to put on a stamp on their letters, sent them to the wrong address, misspelled Brady as Brodie, or posted them by mistake into a rubbish bin. But if even Andrea Jenkyns, the ERG idiot's idiot (a title bitterly contested by Andrew Bridgen), can manage the basics of letter writing then it's safe to assume a group of Tory rebels fuelled largely by fantasy have unsurprisingly turned out to be fantasists.

Either way, the ERG has seemingly managed the impossible. In less than a week, they have made Theresa

May appear vaguely plausible while relegating themselves to an embarrassing, long-past-its-best music hall act. With Rees-Mogg as Archie Rice. In a straight fight between the ERG and *Dad's Army*, Captain Mainwaring would come out on top every time. Tuesday's event had all the feel of the final hurrah before the knacker's yard.

Behind the stage was a placard with the words 'Global Britain'. Global Britain turned out to be seven old, white men waiting for the golf club bar to open. Only the presence of Rees-Mogg brought the average age below 65 and he was feeling every one of his 49 years. Even he never thought he'd sink this low. Whatever would Nanny think?

Peter Lilley, a former trade secretary, got things under way as if he were auditioning for *Dragon's Den*: he had virtually founded the World Trade Organization single-handedly; he was certain everyone was overexaggerating the problems of cross-border trade, as he had once brought a cheese from his second home in France back to the UK without being stopped; no one should worry about Kent becoming a car park as illegal immigrants had already turned it into one; and he'd never come across a trade deal he couldn't negotiate in 10 minutes. Baker perked up at that. Ten minutes probably really meant five. Nothing escaped the numbers man.

The next three nonentity guests had little more to say, other than that they hadn't read the paper but were sure they probably agreed with it. Sir David Ord – me neither

– even managed to do this while appearing to be asleep. The rest of us should have been so lucky. It was left to a dishevelled David Davis to wrap things up. 'I'm overawed to be in such distinguished company,' he began. He really needn't have been. He was perfectly matched, with the stupidity bar set comfortably low.

Much to the panel's disappointment, no one had any questions to ask about Global Britain. Mainly because it was all a rehash of what the ERG had put out several times before and been comprehensively dismissed on every occasion. Instead, everyone wanted to know if the 48 letters were ever going to materialise. Along with the more existential one of why an organisation should have gone to such lengths to prove its lack of credibility. So instead, Lilley recited something from the bible.

Come the end, a scrum rapidly surrounded Rees-Mogg, who did his best to persuade reporters that everything was going totally to plan. Apart from the bits that weren't. The madness becomes ever madder. Even Labour organises better coups than this. Davis tried to use the fracas to escape the scene unnoticed before anyone could ask him if he had written a letter, only to find he had left his briefcase behind a pillar and had to fight his way back in to get it. The end of the end-of-the-pier show.

MPs pile on from all sides to trash May's Brexit non-deal deal

22 NOVEMBER 2018

It was hard to see what all the fuss had been about. The intellectual legend that is David Davis had always said securing a future trade arrangement with the EU would be the easiest deal in the history of David Davis Land. And in the end he was proved right. It was so easy that the government chose not to do anything about it for the best part of two and a half years and then cobbled something together at the last minute.

A day after her brief trip to Brussels, Theresa May came to the Commons to present the deal that she and Jean-Claude Juncker had scribbled down over 26 pages. What she had wasn't a deal exactly – more a vague declaration that things might work out OK at some point over the next 15 years or more. Some things would happen if other unspecified things were also to happen. And if those things weren't to happen, then some other unspecified things would happen as a result.

The prime minister paused, closed her eyes and took a deep breath. Willing herself to believe in what she was saying. Willing herself to be somewhere else. She opened her eyes. It was no good. She was still at the dispatch box. So she ploughed on, her voice becoming ever more dissociated.

She was immensely grateful to Iain Duncan Smith and Owen Paterson for their fascinating and helpful suggestions on Northern Ireland. There was no need for them to worry about the withdrawal agreement because it probably wouldn't be needed. But if it was, there would be no hard border because she had arranged for a First World War blimp to be positioned somewhere in Armagh. Along with an armed, quick-response badger taskforce.

The red lines on red mullet would remain in place. We would be protecting British fisheries by getting rid of the Common Fisheries Policy and replacing it with a Policy of Common Fisheries. Britain would be regaining the right to make its own laws providing that was OK with the European Court of Justice. Then for the coup de grâce. Chequers had been chucked. We wouldn't be getting a Canada deal or a Norway deal. We wouldn't be getting something in between. With luck an Iceland deal. But more likely, and to be more geographically accurate, one that was dead in the water.

This was one of Jeremy Corbyn's easier outings in the Commons. A reply that even he couldn't screw up. Fighting lack of clarity with lack of clarity was his specialism. All he had to do was not fall over, and criticise some bits for not delivering a hard enough Brexit and other bits for not delivering a soft enough Brexit. A little of something for everyone.

May desperately tried to convince the opposition benches that her deal that wasn't a deal met Labour's six tests, which only ended up in a humiliating shout of 'Oh, no it isn't'. Because what the occasion really demanded was for the Commons to degenerate into pantomime.

That, though, was the prime minister's high point, as thereafter MPs from both sides of the house lined up to trash her draft agreement. IDS and Paterson made it clear she had wasted an hour of her time talking to them at Downing Street earlier in the week and that she would have been better off watching *NCIS*. Raab tried and failed to sound as if he wasn't overwhelmed by his own self-importance, while Boris Johnson dismissed her statement for being 'full of generalities and self-contradictions'. Perhaps Boris is more self-aware than any of us thought.

It was almost an hour before May got her first expression of support. And that was only from Damian Green, one of the few people who know her well enough to call her by her first name. Otherwise, it was back to the pile-on. Remainers accused her of betrayal and demanded a second referendum. Brexiters accused her of betrayal and demanded she go back and renegotiate the withdrawal agreement, the only thing that was legally binding and the EU was certain not to change.

Before long, the prime minister was in Maybot mode. 'The backstop was the backstop because it was the backstop that delivered the backstop.' Complete nonsense. She knew it, everyone knew it, but she just couldn't help herself. She was delivering on the deal that was delivering on something that was delivering on something else.

Not so much a political declaration as the martyrdom of St Theresa. The only thing she was delivering was her own head on a plate. In a way, the masochism was almost addictive; when Labour's Helen Goodman inquired if the government was going to follow the procedure committee's advice on a meaningful vote, May was defiant. Why go quietly? She was certain to lose the main vote, so why not lose another?

Denial and bargaining as Theresa May grieves for her Brexit dreams

25 NOVEMBER 2018

More in sorrow than in anger. There were no celebrations, nor even recriminations, as Donald Tusk, Jean-Claude Juncker and Michel Barnier gave their joint press conference at the end of the EU Council meeting in Brussels that had signed off the withdrawal agreement and the draft agreement on the future trading relationship. No great sense of history being made. Just an air of resigned melancholy. That which had been needed to be done had been done. There were no winners. It was a deal that left everyone diminished.

'We will remain friends till the end of days,' said Tusk. 'And one day longer.' But not such close friends as we had once been. Not even friends with benefits. Juncker did see one upside to the whole negotiating process: it had brought the remaining 27 countries together. The EU was more united than before, and would be standing by Spain. Bye bye, Gibraltar.

Now it was up to the UK parliament to see if it wanted to accept it, Barnier observed. Frankly, the EU had already wasted enough headspace on the UK's existential crisis and it wasn't going to take up more of its time trying to second-guess the outcome. As far as he was concerned, that was it. Given Theresa May's self-imposed red lines, the deal on the table was the only one on offer.

More in denial than in sorrow. At her own press conference half an hour later, the British prime minister refused to admit she was sad the UK was leaving the EU. There again, she hardly looked ecstatic at the outcome either. Rather, she appeared broken. A hunched, physically diminished figure peering out over the lectern, looking – as she so often does these days – as if she wished she was somewhere else entirely. Preferably curled up under the duvet, watching old episodes of *NCIS* on her laptop.

Where the EU has moved on to bargaining and depression – the third and fourth stages of grief – May is stuck in the first. Denial. She cannot yet bring herself to admit that her deal is dead in the water. Unloved by everybody. Herself included. There have been no German car manufacturers rushing to her rescue, to thank her for maintaining their access to the UK market. Her dream of a good Brexit deal is dead on arrival.

87

'What the British people want,' the prime minister said time and again, on each occasion mistaking what she herself wanted for what the British people wanted. It was she who was fed up with the whole Brexit process and wanted the whole thing over. It was she who believed it was in the national interest, when everyone could see it was actually only in hers. It was she who wanted to believe in a deal that was so obviously bad for the country, that delivered so little of what had been originally promised. A Brexit deal whose only saving grace was that it would leave everyone marginally better off than leaving the EU with no deal at all.

This was press conference as tragedy. A humiliation that was all the more painful for being obvious to everyone but May, who clung desperately to the hope that somehow her 'people's letter' might head off an inevitable defeat in parliament. That, even if anyone bothered to read her delusional fantasies, they would mistake them for coherent thought and beg their MPs to accept a deal they didn't want. That the collective unconscious would be in favour of self-harm.

Come the questions from the media, there were no straight answers. There seldom are. The denial was still too great. May's eyes deadened and her responses became ever more staccato and evasive. As if her circuit board had been mainlined with Valium. A second-rate Ayn Rand. She wasn't going to think about what would happen if her deal was voted down because she was focused

88

on getting her deal through parliament. She wanted to counsel against the negativity towards a deal about which she herself clearly felt so negative. The power of positive thinking. The triumph of the will, the triumph of the impossible. Yet in ruling nothing in, she was ruling nothing out. All options were still on the table.

And this was all supposed to have been the easy bit. It had taken the best part of two years to reach a withdrawal agreement that no one liked and the vultures would now begin to circle round the future trade arrangements. Spain already had its eyes on Gibraltar and France had its on UK fishing rights. And those were just the easy pickings.

After 10 minutes or so, May scuttled off. This was meant to be a landmark day in Britain's history. A day when the UK had asserted its independence. An occasion to raise a toast to Blighty. So why did it feel like an anti-climax? Why was no one celebrating? Why did she feel so utterly alone? So useless. Grief could do strange things to a person. And a country.

PM's new Brexit mantra: everything is agreed although nothing is agreed

26 NOVEMBER 2018

There are now only two possibilities left. Either no one has told Theresa May the result of last year's general election and she is under the impression she has a 100-seat majority in the Commons. Or she simply cannot count. Whichever it is, we're long past the point where the prime minister's much-prized fortitude and stoicism has slipped into pig-headedness and outright stupidity.

Or possibly madness. If insanity is repeating the same mistake and expecting a different result, then the prime minister is in urgent need of clinical help. Not content with having come to the Commons twice in the past week to give a statement on the Brexit withdrawal agreement and the future declaration, which has been rubbished by almost everyone in Britain, May was back for a third time after the weekend's EU Council meeting to make exactly the same case as before. And to receive precisely the same overwhelmingly hostile reaction.

There was a time when May used to endlessly repeat: 'Nothing is agreed until everything is agreed.' At some point over the past few weeks, her default settings have been rerouted to: 'Everything has been agreed when nothing has been agreed.' No one should get hung up on the backstop arrangements that have been agreed because everyone had privately agreed they should never be used. This was the best deal because it was the only deal. People wanted certainty and she was giving them the guaranteed certainty of prolonged uncertainty. She sat down to near silence from her own benches.

Jeremy Corbyn replied using almost the exact same words he had used in his last two outings at the dispatch box. If the prime minister couldn't be bothered to make an effort, then why should he? Her deal was a bad deal because it delivered a Brexit that was simultaneously too hard and too soft. Sooner or later someone is going to point out to him he can't have it both ways. Or perhaps not. At the moment, all that's required of him is to be one step ahead of May. Something the average 10-year-old can manage.

Then came the inevitable pile-on. From the usual suspects, called by the Speaker in the same predictable order. Iain Duncan Smith, David Davis, Bill Cash and John Redwood. Anna Soubry briefly livened things up by pointing out that, since it was obvious the prime minister's plan stood no chance of getting through parliament, it would be interesting to know if she had a plan B. May was outraged. It had been hard enough work trying to sign off a 600-page document that everyone hated, so expecting her to come up with something that people actually liked was out the question.

Nor was there any respite from the Labour benches as Hilary Benn, Yvette Cooper, Chris Leslie and Rachel Reeves asked questions to which the prime minister had no answer. There was no point in having a second referendum because you couldn't trust the people to come up with the answer you wanted. And it was completely absurd to argue that the UK would be worse off by leaving the EU, because there were so many other ways to measure prosperity than people being broke. Just think of the feelgood factor of dressing in rags. Blessed are the poor, for they shall disinherit Northern Ireland and Gibraltar.

One hour into the statement and not a single MP had spoken in support of her deal. Even Michael Fallon, normally one of May's most loyal of sidekicks, put the boot in. Then Dominic Grieve observed that May's 'People's Letter' was riddled with inaccuracies. May looked bewildered. She'd always assumed the electorate enjoyed being lied to. The first vague hint of support came from Caroline Spelman. Wrong time, wrong person. Spelman is already a dame, so can't be bought off with honours. May passed a note to the chief whip, Julian Smith, most likely a reminder to him to bung a few hundred thousand to Spelman's West Midlands constituency for pothole repairs. Brexit was getting to be an expensive business.

Long before the end, May cut an increasingly isolated and forlorn figure. A prime minister out of time, out of her depth and out of ideas. Praying on a miracle that was never going to come. Going home every evening to curl in a foetal ball, howling a primal scream of despair. Knowing that this was merely the beginning of a two-week period that could only end in humiliation and failure. This time, nothing really had changed. There might not have been a method in her madness. But there sure as hell was a madness in her method.

* * *

In November, the shadow Brexit secretary, Keir Starmer, had used an arcane legal procedure known as a 'humble address' to force the government to publish its full legal advice on the Brexit deal. In particular the advice relating to the Northern Ireland backstop – something the government had been unwilling to disclose. But once it had become clear it was going to be defeated – by the DUP, who had a particular interest in the backstop – the government ordered its own MPs to abstain on the motion. That way hoping the defeat would be seen as something other than a defeat. Despite the loss, the government still didn't publish the advice and it now found itself in contempt of parliament. It was left to the attorney general, Geoffrey Cox, to defend their position. Or not.

Geoffrey Cox milks his moment in Commons spotlight

3 DECEMBER 2018

Boom. The deep baritone of Geoffrey Cox echoed round the chamber. This was the crowning moment of the attorney general's long and extremely well-paid legal career. The number one court at the Old Bailey had nothing on a full house in Westminster. Especially when his back was to the wall defending the near indefensible. These were the days when it was very heaven to be alive. The lights. The greasepaint. The action.

Last month the Commons passed a humble address ordering the government to publish the attorney general's Brexit legal advice and now Cox was in the house to explain in person why he didn't think that was at all a good idea. Boom. Cox began in full Laurence Olivier in Richard III mode. Now was the winter of our discontent made glorious summer by this house of May. There was barely a murmur. He had the audience in his hands from the moment he started speaking.

He had a solemn and constitutional duty, which he would discharge with uncompromising fidelity, he insisted. Indeed, so objective and impartial did he wish to appear that he had gone out of his way to give a 52-page summary of his original six-page legal advice. Almost all of which could already be found in the withdrawal agreement.

'Verily,' he declaimed, sweeping his arms wide open. There were problems with the backstop and on a narrow point of law it could not be ended unilaterally. But, ladies and gentlemen of the jury, it was inconceivable that either the EU and the UK would ever dream of not acting in good faith, and even if one party should – by some mishappenstance – seek to spin out the negotiations beyond 16 years then the whole legality of article 50 would come into question.

The opening soliloquy lasted for a full 18 minutes – most statements are over in 10 at most – and by the end even Cox could see that he was beginning to lose his audience. There was only a certain amount of amateur theatrics that everyone could take – MPs are uniquely averse to others getting too much attention – and when the house lights went up and Cox finally exited stage left, almost no one could remember a word he had said. Which may have been the whole point.

The shadow attorney general, Nick Thomas-Symonds, cut to the chase. He wisely didn't try to out-thesp Cox. Instead he stuck to the basics. The Commons had ordered the government to publish its full legal advice and the government had refused. End of. Cox was in contempt. And while he was about it, could the attorney general list one positive thing about the summary he had given so far?

Boom. 'Mr Speaker,' Cox declared plaintively, dabbing a tear from his eye. 'All he has to do is ask and he shall receive. For I shall answer.' In an instant, he morphed from Olivier to a music hall Henry Irving. A second-rate Victorian actor-manager who was hell-bent on milking the occasion for every last drop of emotion. His hand thudded into the dispatch box, to everyone's general amusement. Cox looked momentarily disconcerted. This was his finest Lear, not his Malvolio.

Boom. Like the old pro that he is, Cox soon regained his composure. On to his Dickens. It is a far, far better thing I do ... There was nothing – NOTHING – he would have loved to have done more than give parliament his full legal advice. But it would be a matter of public harm for him to do so. More than that, it would be against the will of God. Parliament may think it knew best, but it was his sad duty to report that it didn't.

'There is nothing to see here,' he quavered in full am-dram ham. Yes there were risks, but these were mere political – not legal – calculations. The quality of mercy is not strained. Besides, he was just one lawyer among many hundreds. There were many different legal opinions available. Just for a moment, he could almost imagine himself to be a junior barrister defending a shop-lifting charge at Snaresbrook magistrates court, rather than the attorney general. Almost. Cox could never let his extreme self-regard entirely slip.

Cox's perorations didn't begin to satisfy most MPs on both sides and long before the end of his two-and-a-half-hour session he had been given notice that contempt proceedings would be brought against the government. But Cox could live with that. OK, so he normally didn't get out of bed for less than £800 an hour, but so what if he had performed for peanuts? This had been his never-to-be-forgotten masterclass for law-yers and MPs alike. The achievement of a lifetime. His finest hour.

Geoffrey Cox's dreams of an acting career are shattered

4 DECEMBER 2018

As Conservative MPs made their way back into the chamber after voting, Geoffrey Cox sat slumped on the front bench. He'd given his all and it hadn't been enough. Chief whip Julian Smith prodded the attorney general urgently. 'You've still got it, you've still got it,' he said. Cox barely stirred. His West End dreams were in tatters. Now no one would ever see his Lear at the National.

Smith tried again to talk up his man. 'There's always the regions,' he said. He pulled out his phone and started ringing a few repertory companies. His calls went largely unanswered. Thanks, but no thanks. Then the tellers came back and Smith melted away. Cox was on his own. Yesterday the Commons had been his stage, his syrupy baritone projecting into every recess; now he couldn't even get work on an end-of-the-pier show. All that was left was the off-the-end-of-the-pier show.

It wasn't the loss that hurt. Lawyers win and lose day in, day out. It was the shame. It had always been personal for Cox. He'd known he was up against it ever since the hopeless government, of which he had somehow allowed himself to become a part, had been outmanoeuvred by

Labour's humble address forcing the government to publish its Brexit legal advice in full.

But he'd always prided himself on defending the indefensible and he had dared to believe his performance the previous day might have won out. It would have been his finest hour. Never in the whole field of political conflict would so much have been owed by so many to just him. Now he was a broken man. The government had been held in contempt of parliament for the first time in decades and his assurances to the Commons that there had never been anything to hide had not been accepted.

The writing had been on the wall ever since the Speaker had allowed Labour to table a contempt motion. Shadow Brexit secretary Keir Starmer is no mean lawyer himself, and he opened the debate with forensic brevity. This was an open and shut case. Parliament had instructed the government to publish its legal advice and it had refused. Indeed, in one of the attorney general's many soliloquies the night before, Cox had all but admitted he was bang to rights himself. Now was the time for him and the government to be held to account.

There are few people anyone would want defending them less than Andrea Leadsom. The leader of the House has always made a virtue out of being out of her depth, and she excelled herself by failing to understand any of the legal arguments. Even though the attorney general had written to the Speaker, saying he had been unable to comply with the humble address because its remit had been too vague, Leadsom insisted he had no case to answer because he had fulfilled all the demands made upon him. So couldn't everyone do the decent thing and just kick the motion into the long grass? Cox glanced to his right, raised his eyes and groaned.

The DUP's Nigel Dodds all but sealed the government's fate by declaring that he would be voting with the opposition. It was a matter of principle. The attorney general couldn't have it both ways. He couldn't argue that it would not be in the national interest for his advice to be published and still insist that it contained nothing of any interest that he hadn't already disclosed.

From then on it was all downhill, as first William Cash sucked all the life out of the Commons with an unintelligible ramble and then Nadine Dorries stood up to share some thoughts. Thinking isn't Dorries's strong point, and her conclusion that Cox was basically a civil servant was just another nail in his coffin. By way of a finale, a succession of Tory lobby fodder no-hopers – to call them second-rate would be to flatter them – tried to waste time as the government whips scoured Westminster for the necessary votes. Which they never found.

Having just lost two unnecessary votes, the government achieved the hat-trick when Dominic Grieve's amendment, to allow parliament a meaningful vote if the prime minister's Brexit deal did not survive contact with the Commons, was passed. So it was a battered

Theresa May who eventually opened the Brexit debate some five hours later than scheduled. It was intended to be a hard sell, but her heart just wasn't in it. Rather, it had the tinge of sadness. An eye on her legacy rather than the future. A farewell to the main stage. Cox knew just how she felt. All was chaos. Entropy! Entropy! Everyone's got it entropy!

Corbyn gives May unexpected lifeline but Javid flounders

5 DECEMBER 2018

Three defeats inside 63 minutes in the Commons. A government found to be in contempt of parliament for the first time in living memory. The prime minister's desperate efforts to turn the Brexit vote into a binary choice between her deal and no deal nullified by Dominic Grieve's amendment. If Theresa May had had worse nights, she couldn't immediately remember them.

Nor was her mood improved the following morning when she was reluctantly forced to publish the attorney general's legal advice. Geoffrey Cox's insistence that there wasn't anything to see in it had turned out to be a bit of a porky. No one could remember him telling the Commons that the Northern Ireland backstop might be 'indefinite' or that trade talks could end in 'stalemate'.

So it was a decidedly shaky-looking May who entered the chamber for an hour of prime minister's questions she could have done without.

But then a stroke of luck. It turned out that the only person in the entire country to be unaware the government was on its last legs was the leader of the opposition. Let's talk about austerity, Jeremy Corbyn began. May blinked once. Then twice. Just to check she hadn't died and gone to heaven. But no. She was still breathing and the Labour leader really had forgotten to mention Brexit. And that she had no majority without the DUP. And that she would be lucky to last another fortnight.

'We are making changes to the changes we are making,' May replied, wrong-footed by Corbyn's amnesia and playing for time as she tried to regain her composure. The Labour leader showed no sign of realising the prime minister was talking nonsense and just kept his head down and stuck to the script.

Unbelievably, that opening exchange turned out to have been the intellectual highpoint, and thereafter May and Corbyn failed to land a single punch. It was real bottom-of-the-bill entertainment. If that was a taster of a forthcoming general election leader's debate it will be a ratings disaster. Give me a load of chimps killing one another any day. It would up the IQ levels by several points.

Sajid Javid had an altogether rougher ride when the second day of the Brexit debate got under way around lunchtime. The home secretary is not short on self-regard and likes to consider himself one of the frontrunners to replace May when she finally gets round to doing the decent thing. But even he knows that the prime minister's deal is a complete shambles and has no chance of getting though the Commons and his performance at the dispatch box reflected his lack of confidence in his own brief.

'Um, er,' he mumbled, refusing to make eye contact with anyone. Um, er, basically the deal was a bit rubbish and the country's security would be compromised a bit but, all in all, there probably wouldn't to too many unnecessary deaths and he couldn't think of anything better.

Within 30 seconds of him starting his speech, at least half a dozen MPs from both sides of the house were piling in with their interventions. Javid ripped off his shirt and surrendered willingly to the onslaught. Northern Ireland would be remaining under the jurisdiction of the EU, the DUP's Nigel Dodds barked. There was no mention of the international databases, SIS II or Ecris, in any of the draft agreements, Yvette Cooper, chair of the home affairs select committee observed.

As the arrows rained down on him, Javid looked more and more miserable. There had to be better ways of earning a living than being home secretary for a government this useless. Yes, the deal was no more than a Santa wishlist, he burbled. But couldn't everyone just hope for the best and hope that crims spontaneously decided to hand themselves in because they were so thrilled to be free from the jurisdiction of the EU.

'Nnnnnnnnationnn,' whispered Javid. He was urged to speak up by the 100 or so MPs who had stayed to torment him. 'Nnnnnnnnationnn,' he said again. It gradually dawned on everyone that the subject the home secretary was trying not to talk about was immigration. Simply because he had nothing to say. The government's immigration white paper that had been first promised more than a year ago was still unwritten. So he had no idea what the government's policy actually was. Other than that some bits would be the same, others would be a bit different and they hoped to get rid of a few foreigners.

Cooper observed that only a couple of weeks previously, he had promised her committee the white paper would be available before next Tuesday's vote. Was he going back on that? 'Possibly,' Javid replied sulkily. Possibly, as in yes. It would definitely come by the end of December. December 2020.

The end of days draws nigh – our Maybot's gone truly rogue

6 DECEMBER 2018

For a while now, some of us in Westminster have been convinced that Theresa May is a sleeper agent whose

103

mission is to undermine her own government. That conspiracy theory is now officially dead in the water. Because there is now nothing secretive about the prime minister's actions. Her cover is well and truly blown. She is entirely open about using every opportunity to destroy her credibility.

May has gone rogue. A one-woman Terminator whose systems are riddled with malware and who is hellbent on destroying everything around her. The government, the country, the universe. But most of all, herself.

It's long been axiomatic that the prime minister is at her most convincing when she is saying nothing at all. So her best chance of getting her Brexit deal through the Commons was always to hide under the duvet and watch *Dynasties* on her laptop.

But at some point in the last few days, May has appeared to come to the astonishing conclusion that she actually has a hope of winning next Tuesday's vote. Quite how she has come to that algorithmic impossibility is not clear – circuit overload is the most likely answer – but now the idea is in her head she is doing everything in her power to make sure it doesn't become reality. Which is why she chose to spend her breakfast time giving a 20-minute interview to Radio 4's *Today* programme.

Here was the prime minister at her most Maybotic. Staccato, brittle and with a delivery that flatlined. She could not have sounded less enthusiastic about her deal if she had tried. It was a good deal because it was the only deal, she said in a dead monotone.

Worried that she might be presenting herself as too coherent, May spent the last 15 minutes failing to give straight answers to straight questions, talking in meaningless soundbites and leaving everyone guessing as to whether she really had a strategy. If there had been anyone in favour of her deal at the start of the interview, there wasn't by the end.

Further evidence of May's masterplan to undermine the country was on show at Brexit questions in the Commons. In its early days the Brexit department had a sense of national importance. Now it is nothing more than a sideshow, whose primary job is to try to make sure there are enough lorry parks in Kent in case the country grinds to a standstill on 30 March next year.

Having already lost two Brexit secretaries in David Davis and Dominic Raab – no great loss, some might say – May has had to rustle up someone else to do the job.

It hasn't been easy. The Four Pot Plants declined to join the cabinet on the grounds that they were hopelessly overqualified. So the prime minister had to cast her net wider. In Stephen Barclay she made an inspired choice. Barclay is a man after her own heart. A man who can spend hours saying nothing meaningful. Though in his case he has little alternative as he doesn't actually know anything meaningful. He is the nonentity's nonentity. Brexit questions passed in a gentle haze of futility, while the few dozen MPs in the chamber dozed off. The radio-active isotopes Barclay is tasked with stockpiling have a longer half-life than his department.

In the third day of the Brexit debate, Philip Hammond was talking down both the deal and the economy. He was very keen to keep his distance from the withdrawal agreement and future partnership by repeatedly referring to the deal as 'the prime minister's deal'. Nothing to do with me, guv. It was basically all a bit rubbish and everyone was going to be broke, but we'd be a bit less broke with 'the prime minister's' deal. Thanks.

There were many interventions. Quite why Nadine Dorries is so keen to parade her ignorance is a mystery – you'd have thought she'd have preferred to leave room for doubt – and Hammond only made half-hearted attempts to defend the deal. The forecasts predicting doom weren't forecasts. They were modelled scenarios that predicted doom. That sort of thing.

Like the rest of the government, Hammond seems more concerned with considering his own future rather than the country's after the vote is lost next Tuesday.

John McDonnell gave a measured and reasoned deconstruction of why the government's deal was a total mess. He rather glossed over the fact that the Labour leadership had yet to come up with their own plan that didn't presuppose the EU would give us all the benefits of being in the customs union and single market with none of the obligations.

Even so, the shadow chancellor's contribution was rather more helpful than much of what followed. The nadir was David Davis, who knows even less about the economy than he does about anything else. His main thrust was that he had been absolutely right to do nothing as Brexit secretary because EU negotiations always got done in the last 10 seconds, and that Canada +++ was called Canada +++ because it delivered Canada − − −. Truly we are reaching the end of days.

Laws of Maybotics collapse in PM's theatre of the absurd

10 DECEMBER 2018

Shortly after lunch, Graham Brady received another letter of no confidence in the prime minister. This one was from the Four Pot Plants. Enough was enough. The laws of Maybotics had finally collapsed in on themselves. Theresa May had backed herself into a corner in which every course of action ended in extreme self-harm.

In the morning May had sent Michael Gove out on to Radio 4's *Today* programme to insist that Tuesday's vote on the government's Brexit deal would go ahead as planned. Hours later, her spokesperson made the same assurances to lobby journalists. Within minutes, it was announced that the prime minister had changed her mind. The deal that had previously been not just the right deal but also the only deal on the table had turned out to be the wrong deal and there was another one on offer after all. Maybe.

'I've listened very carefully,' May said to widespread laughter at the opening of her statement to the Commons on her volte-face. And the person she had been listening to was her chief whip. The numbers were terrible. She wasn't just going to lose the vote she was going to be totally humiliated. So she had chosen to do what she always does in such circumstances. She had swapped one humiliation for another. Who cared if the pound tanked and the stock market crashed, just so long as she could defer some of the pain for a later date? Masochism can do strange things to a person.

Having explained why everything had changed, May retreated into her default coping mechanism: denial. It was almost too excruciatingly painful to watch. The disintegration of a prime minister, a country turned into an international laughing stock. Nothing had changed. Nothing had changed. Her deal was still exactly the right deal apart from the bits that weren't quite right. And what she was planning to do was to go back to the EU in the hope of getting a few more commas, that had no legal authority, inserted into the future declaration. Anything to buy time.

Nothing had changed. Nothing had changed. It had never been her intention to hold a vote on Tuesday because Tuesday had been cancelled and tomorrow was now officially going to be declared to be Wednesday. Apart from anything else, it had come to her attention that many MPs had been working very hard of late and she wanted to give them a day off either to watch Parliament TV on catchup TV – who wouldn't want to watch reruns of a three-day debate that had been totally pointless? – or to do their Xmas shopping. No one could accuse May of being reluctant to put her lack of credibility on the line.

For once, Jeremy Corbyn was heard in silence. Not just because he was more forensic than usual in his dismantling of the prime minister's insistence that she was planning to renegotiate something the EU had already said was non-negotiable, but also because MPs on all sides were still reeling from May's opening statement. Either her systems were now malfunctioning so badly she couldn't help contradicting herself, or she had finally lost all sense of shame. And self-respect. Even the mirror could no longer look her in the face.

The Speaker intervened to observe that it would be a pathetic show of weakness for the government to unilaterally pull the vote rather than to allow the Commons to have a say on pulling the vote. May visibly shrank into the front bench, shaking her head furiously and willing herself to disappear into the green leather. If she couldn't win a meaningful vote she didn't stand a prayer of winning a vote on not holding a vote.

It soon became clear that May's dadaist theatre of the absurd had only succeeded in changing one person's mind. Before her babbles of mindlessnessnessness, Kenneth Clarke had indicated he was prepared to vote with the government. Now he had withdrawn his consent. Shitshow didn't begin to cover today's proceedings. This was an embarrassment on a truly global scale. Something even Donald Trump would have difficulty explaining away. Every other MP merely repeated their previous opinions. May was still staring vacantly at defeat.

Not that she cared. By now she had gone entirely rogue, making up policy on the hoof. She even declared it had never been her intention to hold the vote the following day and that 21 January had been the key date. Even the cabinet looked embarrassed by this. There was only one explanation that now made sense. The prime minister had taken a huge bet with Paddy Power on her still being in a job by Christmas. She just hadn't read the small print. When the fun stops, stop.

Tory headbangers save the Maybot – for the time being at least

12 DECEMBER 2018

Milking his brief moment in the limelight, Graham Brady, the chairman of the 1922 Committee, announced that Theresa May had won the no confidence vote by 200 votes to 117. Hardly emphatic, but it would do. She could stay for the time being. It came as no real surprise. A party that can barely govern the country could hardly have been expected to mount an effective leadership challenge. The European Research Group had gambled and lost, its longed-for saviour, Boris Johnson, not so much Aslan as Cecil the Lion. A rotting trophy on an American dentist's wall.

Inside a sweaty committee room 14, Tory MPs – all except Chris Grayling, who managed to turn up 20 minutes late – had banged the tables when the prime minister arrived. With their heads. May has that effect on people. 'Good morning,' she said. Not the best of starts, given the time was 5pm. 'I've been very clear,' she continued, wisely choosing to keep her appeal short and sweet.

So clear, that by the time everyone left an hour later no one could exactly remember what she had said. 'She said she was very clear,' said James Cleverly, scratching his head. Almost everyone had a slightly different version. Some thought she had promised to go soon, others only that she would be gone by 2022. She probably didn't know which herself. Classic Maybot.

It wasn't that anyone had thought May was doing a particularly good job; more that finding a suitable replacement at this particular time was too much hassle. Even the prime minister had accepted she wasn't really up to it. Just a bit longer, she had begged. Pretty please. Only her assurances that she wouldn't lead the party into another election had secured the necessary votes to get her over the line. And given her past record on keeping her promises, who could possibly disbelieve her? The Tories are nothing if not gullible.

Cabinet colleagues who had spent the past few months plotting their own leadership bids suddenly rallied round, professing their undying love and support. 'She's the best,' Amber, Sajid and Jeremy had gasped in rapture to any broadcaster that would have them. Kissy, kissy. A little extra time to finesse their campaigns and allow Theresa to take the hit for a crap Brexit deal or a second referendum wouldn't be the end of the world.

Just another day in the shitshow Brexitland hell. A government that has been found in contempt of parliament. An opposition that doesn't really know how to oppose. A country burning in front of everyone's eyes and a Tory party only interested in tearing itself apart. Even Sartre might have raised a grudging smile at the universality of such existential futility.

At the centre of it all was the prime minister. A woman who is visibly disappearing before her own eyes. Her reflection rapidly fading in the mirror. Hunched, cowered and a hostage to her own stubbornness. The police who are on guard in Downing Street have failed miserably in preventing her from committing self-harm. Not to mention national harm.

May's morning hadn't got off to the best of starts with the announcement the ERG had finally managed to count up to 48 and rapidly went downhill with an endorsement from David Cameron, tweeting from the comfort of his

£25,000 shed. The last thing she needed was the support of someone even more useless than her. Just. The battle to be the UK's worst post-war prime minister is going down to the wire. Her car couldn't even get into the Commons at the first attempt as the gates were locked and she had to circle Westminster Square. The second time in two days when she'd been trapped in a back seat. Write your own metaphors. These are the moments when you realise you'd have been better off staying in bed.

Not for the first time, prime minister's questions provided May with 45 minutes' respite. Anyone visiting from another planet might have thought the UK was in robust shape, rather than staggering towards self-immolation. Jeremy Corbyn had begun in shouty mode – someone must have been tampering with his allotment – but the Labour leader seemed genuinely unaware there was a Tory leadership contest going on. It's almost as if his body clock is set 48 hours behind everyone else's. As an Arsenal fan, he's going to be mighty pissed off when he finds out that Spurs drew with Barcelona.

All that was required of May was to appear vaguely sentient. As her husband twitched nervously in the public gallery, watching what could have been her final PMQs, the prime minister barely rose above standby mode. She failed to realise the reason no one laughed at her joke was not because they hadn't understood it, but because it wasn't funny. She monotoned her usual responses to questions that hadn't been asked. Her Brexit deal was going just brilliantly. Thank you and good night. I'll be here all week. And possibly longer.

All the while, chief whip Julian Smith was nose down, checking his phone. Counting the numbers. Counting, counting. Andrew Griffiths looked thrilled to receive a message saying he could vote for Theresa. There was nothing he liked more than having the whip restored. The harder the better.

And that was that. It might be undemocratic for the country to have a second referendum but it was just fine for the Tories to have another leadership election within two years. Today wasn't a day to worry about hypocrisy. Today was the day to celebrate just clinging on.

The reality was that nothing had changed. Nothing had changed. May's Brexit deal was no more likely to get through the Commons than it had been before the vote. If anything positions had hardened. The EU would not be coming to her rescue. All the future offered was more deadlock, more division. Dante was wrong. There was a tenth circle of hell and we were in it. Government as mindless light entertainment.

* * *

At yet another EU summit over the weekend of 13–14 December, Theresa May maintained that she had been 'crystal clear' with the 27 other European leaders about the assurances she needed on the Northern Ireland backstop to get it through the British parliament. The EU seemed to have found her anything but clear. No one appeared to be any the wiser about what tweaks could be made to the withdrawal deal and Jean-Claude Juncker declared the UK position to be nebulous. The EU Commission president, Donald Tusk, insisted there could be no more negotiation to the withdrawal treaty given the red lines the UK government had itself set and pointed out that the EU had treated the British prime minister with a great deal more respect than her own MPs. All in all, not a resounding success.

Shortly afterwards, May announced that she would be stepping down before the next general election. Typically, this raised as many questions as answers. What Tory MPs really wanted to know was just when the next election was going to be and how soon before it she would be standing down. Under the fixed-term parliament act, the next election wasn't due to take place till June 2022. The idea of May hanging on for another three years was not exactly the olive branch most Tory MPs had been hoping to be given.

Parliament begins to eat itself with no Brexit resolution on horizon

18 DECEMBER 2018

We've reached the point where only four diagnoses are now left. The prime minister is in a delusional, psychotic state and is in urgent need of help. Or the prime minister is focused purely on her own short-term survival: even she can't be so far gone as to believe she has a long-term future. Or the prime minister is a sleeper agent for a hostile government committed to the destruction of the UK. Or the prime minister is totally incompetent.

Examine the evidence of the last few weeks. First, she is incapable of keeping almost every commitment she gives: it is now safer to plan for the opposite of what she says will happen. Then she goes to the EU summit and manages to come away with an even worse deal than the already bad one she had secured.

And now she has announced the government will be spending £4 billion in preparing for a no-deal Brexit that it openly admits it doesn't want and would be extremely damaging. So rather than do the obvious thing of ruling it out and donating the spare cash to building several hospitals, Theresa May has got Chris 'Failing' Grayling to book extra lorry spaces on cross-Channel ferries and man-boy Matt Hancock to buy a load of fridges in the Curry's sale. Too little and too late, but all in the faint hope of scaring MPs into voting for her lame-duck deal.

What's left is paralysis. In the absence of a meaningful vote – why would you want to spoil Christmas when there are still over 100 days to go before the UK leaves the EU? – parliament has been reduced to filling the dead air with meaningless debate. Not that many MPs necessarily object to that, as there is nothing they like more than to be given the chance to repeat the same thing they said the day before at greater length, but it doesn't do much for anyone's self-esteem. Despair hangs like a choking smog in Westminster.

There are few cabinet ministers better suited to acts of extreme pointlessness than Gavin Williamson. The defence secretary makes Hancock look positively statesmanlike, so it was entirely fitting he was sent out to waste an hour of everyone's time with a statement on his much-delayed report into modernising Britain's defence capabilities. A report that ran to all of 28 pages, including 10 pages of adverts for photos of Airfix models that Williamson needed to complete his collection.

Please take me seriously, pleaded Private Pike as MPs on both sides of the house started sniggering. No one could. No one ever can. Not even his own family. In desperation, Williamson started threatening to unleash 3,500 troops as part of his department's contingency plans for a no-deal Brexit. They'll shoot to kill any Jerries that get in their way, Pike shouted. Don't mention the war! Labour's shadow defence secretary, Nia Griffith, gently reminded him that the 3,500 troops in his playpen were actually made of plastic.

As there wasn't much else left for it to do, parliament began to eat itself. The shadow leader, Valerie Vaz, understandably cringed as she was instructed by Jeremy Corbyn to raise a point of order to ask why the government had failed to react meaningfully to Labour's futile gesture of a meaningless expression of no confidence in the prime minister, at which point the SNP's Angus Brendan MacNeil raised a second point of order asking if he could table a vote of no confidence in the opposition. Several Labour MPs looked happy to back that one.

Then came a three-hour emergency debate to give MPs yet another chance to debate Brexit. Just as they had done the day before. And the day before that. What they weren't going to get was any resolution. This was more some kind of Brexit Anonymous group therapy session.

'My name's Ian and I'm a Brexit addict,' said the SNP leader Ian Blackford.

'Hi Ian,' everyone replied.

'It's all shit and I feel completely powerless over Brexit,' Blackford said.

'Thank you for sharing. My name's Stephen Bartley ...' said the Brexit secretary.

'It's an anonymous programme. But your name is Stephen Barclay,' the Speaker interrupted.

'Is it? My name's Stephen and my job is to know nothing about anything.'

'You're doing brilliantly,' everyone said encouragingly. Bartley beamed. He was never happier than when even he didn't know who he was.

'My name's Keir and I am embarrassed that Labour is in such a mess over Brexit and is unable to provide any opposition,' said Keir Starmer. 'I wish I wasn't here.' A sentiment with which everyone could agree.

* * *

Brexit was briefly forgotten during the last prime minister's questions before Christmas, when television footage of the session appeared to catch Jeremy Corbyn mouthing the words 'stupid woman' about Theresa May. The Commons descended into near anarchy as Tory MPs tried to raise points of order about the Labour leader's apparent misogyny. Andrea Leadsom upped the ante by reminding the speaker, John Bercow, that he had also once called her a stupid woman. Bercow insisted he could not give a ruling as he had not seen the incident. Corbyn's advisers later briefed the media that what he had actually said was 'stupid people' and was referring to the entire Tory party. The fact that it may have looked like he was saying 'woman' was because he had downloaded some YouTube ventriloquism videos and that if you stuck your tongue behind your teeth then a P could appear a bit like a W. Sadly, the message got through to Barry Gardiner a bit too late and he had already told everyone on national TV that Jeremy had said 'stupid woman'. Bazza would be in for a kicking later.

The row rumbled on for a couple of days and only died down when the Conservative party deftly restored the party whip to two backbenchers who had allegedly been involved in sex scandals, in order to give the government some much-needed extra votes in the forthcoming Brexit debates. The 17-day Christmas recess couldn't come soon *enough for a government that had had a 2018 it would rather forget. Theresa May just hoped her MPs used the break wisely and took so many drugs they would forget all the reasons they objected to her Brexit deal. There was still time for one more calamity, though. Step Forward Chris 'Failing' Grayling, who managed to keep Gatwick airport, which had been shut down by an unidentified drone, closed for longer than necessary by refusing all offers of help from military anti-drone units. It turned out that Grayling was only warming up for greater incompetencies to follow.*

Failing Grayling is a method loser worthy of an Oscar

8 JANUARY 2019

Here's a thought. If Chris Grayling didn't exist, would you be able to create him? Would you dare imagine a government minister who was quite so dim and obviously out of his depth? Or would you fear that if you did, no one would believe you?

When Theresa May appointed Grayling as transport secretary, she did so in the belief she was sidelining him into a job in which he could do little damage. Put him in charge of the NHS and half the country might have died within a matter of months, but surely the worst he could do at transport was make a few trains run late or fail to build the odd roundabout outside Kettering.

Wrong. Like all of us, the prime minister severely underestimated Grayling's capacity for failure. He treats failing as a serious piece of living theatre. There are no half measures with our Chris. He is a method loser. A perfectionist who should have won countless Oscars by now.

From the second he wakes up to the final moments before he falls asleep at night, Grayling dedicates himself to doing everything badly. Not just a bit badly, but completely and utterly uselessly. He is hellbent on being the worst iteration of himself he can possibly be. If he weren't in charge of a government department, such single-mindedness would be almost admirable.

Not that there aren't still some finishing touches to be made. Grayling can just about walk without falling over. If by walking, you count a lumbering plod. He can also talk. Though only as a stream of unconsciousness. He has long since lost the capacity for coherent thought.

Grayling's only outward sign of sentience is a twitch in his left cheek, and this nervous tic was in evidence well before he was called upon to answer an urgent question about his decision to award a £13.8 million contract to a ferry company with no ferries. The cheek is Grayling's last remaining centre of intelligent life: when it wobbles, it's a sure sign he's in danger. Even though he isn't aware of it himself.

Rather, he expressed surprise that anyone should doubt his ability to plan for a no-deal Brexit. As far as he was concerned, the fact everything was taking place at the last minute was an indication of just how advanced his preparations were. He even cited the previous day's abject failure to create a pretend lorry jam as evidence of his success. It's one thing to humiliate yourself. It's quite another not to even realise you are doing it.

The shadow transport secretary, Andy McDonald, looked vaguely bemused. What bit of Seaborne Ferries having no ferries, no money and no website other than a pizza menu didn't Failing Grayling understand? Even the mayor of Ostend had already said the ferry service wouldn't be allowed into his port. Why had no due diligence been done?

'I make no apologies,' Grayling insisted. It was typical of Labour to nitpick. Since when did a ferry company actually need any ships? Seaborne was actually working on a Lego catapult to throw lorries from Ramsgate across to Belgium. And complaining about directors having racked up debts in previous ventures was just anti-business. He was sick and tired of people talking down bankruptcy.

While Grayling was busy embarrassing himself, the Conservative stooge James Heappey was handing out crib sheets to backbenchers, begging them to ask vaguely supportive questions of the transport secretary. Bernard

Jenkin, eager to live down to his portrayal in James Graham's Channel 4 Brexit drama as an establishment buffoon, was the first on his feet to congratulate Grayling for all his hard work and observe that it was totally unfair to expect him to know anything about Seaborne. Charlie Elphicke agreed, suggesting Labour was only interested in wrecking and sabotage tactics.

Too late. Grayling was more than capable of wrecking and sabotaging his own position without any help from Labour. First, he said it didn't matter if Seaborne ran any ferries or not, because if they didn't then they wouldn't get the £13.8 million anyway. This silenced many Tories, because even they could understand that the logic of contingency planning based on a ferry company not delivering additional capacity was inherently flawed. But not Failing Grayling. He was on a roll. His one regret was that he hadn't awarded even more worthless contracts.

The failure was complete. Grayling had yet again died on his feet. It's what he does. A kinder prime minister would have removed him long ago, but he serves a purpose in making others look less mediocre. So he lived to lose another day. Besides, he had a relaxing afternoon ahead flying his drone near Heathrow.

Tory Brexiters are calling for his head. Bercow is in his element

9 JANUARY 2019

Seven former Speakers of the House of Commons have been executed. To judge by the looks on the faces of many on the government benches, John Bercow came dangerously close to becoming the eighth. For well over an hour of points of order that came dangerously close to outright entropy, Tory MPs were spitting blood about the Speaker's decision to allow an amendment by the Conservative Dominic Grieve to force the government to have a vote on a Brexit plan B within three days if its plan A was rejected next Tuesday.

Cue absolute scenes. Constitutional outrage, yelled many MPs, working themselves up into an unpleasant shade of purple. A curious description of what appeared to most normal people as a relatively minor disagreement over parliamentary procedures. The cartoon Brexiter Mark Francois was particularly apoplectic. It was all a stitch-up. Bercow was a Remainer to his core and he had only granted the amendment in the hope of making a no-deal less likely.

Bercow was in his element, becoming ever more pompous and self-important in his mannerisms. Francois had been right to say that the original motion said no motion could be moved other than by a minister of the crown, but this was an amendment that didn't need to be debated. So tough. If the Commons didn't like the amendment then it could always vote it down. Not that it would, because Bercow wasn't stupid enough to select a contentious amendment that wouldn't get passed. The government's real problem wasn't the amendment; it was its lack of a majority.

'This is just sophistry,' huffed Francois. It was nothing more than a total abuse of all that was good and pure about Commons procedure. Bercow beamed. The session was going even better than he had dared hope. There was nothing he liked more than being the centre of attention. This was to be the day when he extended his powers a little further.

Labour MPs weren't slow to come up with points of order of their own. Either to congratulate the Speaker for his singular display of judgment and brilliance; or to observe that it was a sweet irony that many Tories, who had made taking back control of the sovereignty of the British parliament the defining slogan of the Leave campaign, were now so upset that the legislature was being handed greater control over the executive.

Be careful what you wish for. A few assorted opposition MPs were so mesmerised by proceedings that all they could do was stand up, make points of order demanding other people would stop standing up to make points of order so the Commons could get on with its business. Much more of this and we'd have disappeared through the looking glass. Not so much about taking back control as needing to get a sodding grip.

While all this was going on, the chief whip, Julian Smith, was busy punching texts into his phone and wondering what on earth he had done in a previous life to deserve his current one. He had lost a vote yesterday and he was now certain to lose another one today. He would also lose the Brexit vote next Tuesday and now the one the following week. Not least because there was no plan B to have a vote on. Come to think of it, there was barely a plan A. Whips were supposed to win votes, not lose them. He was becoming the Thinking Man's Chris Grayling.

'Just do something,' he hissed to Andrea Leadsom, the leader of the house. Leadsom obliged by asking Bercow if he had consulted the clerks and, if so, whether they had agreed with his judgment. The Speaker confirmed he had consulted them but refused to divulge the contents of their conversation.

Then would he care to publish the clerk's advice, Leadsom enquired, nudging the irony meters even further into the red as the government had spent the last two years trying to prevent details of any of its Brexit analysis and negotiations from being made public. Bercow beamed. If it was all the same to the house, he'd rather keep his discussions private.

He shrugged. He knew he was winging it a bit, but what the hell? He was on a roll and he'd got away with it so far. What was the purpose of precedent, if not to be broken from time to time? Hell, if everything had stayed the same since the middle ages, he'd have been a dead man long ago. And if he could do his bit to save the country from a no-deal Brexit then so much the better.

On and on it went. Jacob Rees-Mogg made a point that was only intelligible to him and was almost certainly incorrect, while Crispin Blunt accused Bercow of outright bias and urged him to stand down. No chance. Bercow had the numbers, as the vote on the amendment would prove.

Despairing May treads water before the main event

14 JANUARY 2019

Naught's had, all's spent. Theresa May tried. She really tried. But she just couldn't manage it. The toxic mix of Brexit and her own stubborn incompetence has corroded the prime minister from the inside, and now she's little more than a fragile shell. Unable to do much more than mechanically go through the motions in pursuit of a vote that she knows to be unwinnable. Sartre would have killed to know such existential despair.

The Conservatives also recognise the game is up and that their leader's authority is little more than an illusion. For May's last-ditch effort to persuade the unpersuadable with a statement to the Commons, there were huge gaps on the government benches. Partly because few Tory MPs had anything to gain from putting themselves through such a numbing experience, but mostly to save themselves from having to witness a prime minister's suffering. It was that painful to watch.

Glassy-eyed and shrunken, May retreated into her familiar safe place. A hurried, disengaged monotone. A phoned-in repetition of every other Brexit statement she had given over the past few months. She didn't believe a word of what she was saying, but she was nothing if not dutiful. She had some letters from the EU. Letters that were elegantly written and contained no spelling mistakes, but sadly lacked anything legally binding on the Northern Ireland backstop.

After admitting that she had basically wasted the past five weeks by delaying the vote, the prime minister went on to make an unusual pitch. Remainer MPs should vote for her deal because if they didn't then they would increase the likelihood of a no-deal Brexit, and Leavers should vote for her deal because a failure to do so would increase the likelihood of no Brexit at all. Even a dodgy 1980s Amstrad computer would have detected that contradiction in its algorithms.

May left her greatest misjudgment to the end, by reminding MPs that history would judge them. This from a government that had mishandled the Brexit negotiations from the off, had awarded a ferry contract to a company with no ferries, whose defence secretary wants to paintball the Spanish and whose international trade secretary believes that a no-deal Brexit wouldn't be as bad as Dunkirk. Great. At least we won't be dive-bombed by Stukas on the beach. History certainly will judge this government and the verdict won't be kind.

In a parallel universe, Jeremy Corbyn and Theresa May might have been an ideal match on a blind date. Both have a flair for the mediocre and instinctively misjudge the mood of the house. The Labour leader said all the right things in reply – the deal she was offering was exactly the same as the one the house would have rejected in December, etc. – but he did so with little grace. This was a time for calm, measured, statesmanlike Jeremy. Not shouty, snarky Jeremy. For someone who is hoping to engineer a general election, he made little effort to engage those voters he needs to win over to become prime minister.

As so often, the two leaders set the tone for what followed. Even normally passionate speakers such as Ken Clarke, Anna Soubry and Ed Miliband sounded as if they were overwhelmed with the semi-detached ennui of déjà vu. Everything that needed to be said had been said months ago. Along with a lot that hadn't needed to be said and had been said anyway. Step forward Owen Paterson, who yet again insisted that the Northern Ireland border could be solved by imaginary technology operated by badgers.

Several MPs from both sides of the house pressed May on whether she would extend article 50. Naturally, she prevaricated, because that's what she always does. It's her default mode. It's one of the reasons the country is so screwed. Plaid Cymru's Liz Saville-Roberts injected some edge into the debate by observing that May hadn't been so insistent on respecting the will of the people when the Welsh voted in favour of having their own national assembly, but the moment quickly passed. The time for home truths was long over.

Then we were back to treading water. Monday was just a sideshow, with Tuesday's vote the main event. Only then would we begin to see if the government did have a plan B, or whether the only contingency was to repeat plan A and hope for a different result. A plan that in the real world might be called the definition of insanity, but in the fantasy world of Westminster is increasingly viewed as a viable option. Brexit is making fools of everyone. Especially those who were already fools in the first place.

The Maybot, zen-like, finds comfort in the certainty of defeat

15 JANUARY 2019

We should never have doubted her. Even after her government had suffered the most humiliating defeat on record, there was only the slightest chink in the prime minister's denial. After seizing the initiative by volunteering to accept a motion of no confidence the next day and insisting she would listen to parliament and reach out to other parties, Theresa May retreated into her shell. Something would happen sooner or later but she had no idea what. All along, the plan B had been to have no plan B and try to muddle along with plan A. Give May enough time and a version of plan A could even be back on the table.

Jeremy Corbyn duly tabled his vote of no confidence and the SNP's Ian Blackford and Labour's Yvette Cooper implored the prime minister to extend article 50. May remained impassive, giving nothing away. Almost zen-like. The most painful bit had been the waiting to lose the vote. Sitting and wondering if it would be as bad as she feared. In hindsight, she now regretted delaying the vote as it had rather ruined her Christmas. Now it was over she felt an unexpected serenity. She was still alive. She was still breathing. The country might be in chaos but she felt weirdly OK.

Making her closing statement, May had been consumed by fear. She knew she was supposed to be making a rousing last-ditch appeal to parliament, but she'd never been able to lift herself above autopilot. Her delivery was flat and disengaged as she ran through the reasons why parliament should accept her deal for the umpteenth time. It offered certainty. The certainty of defeat. It was the most important vote in MPs' lives. Until tomorrow's.

Or the day after. Tomorrow and tomorrow and tomorrow. At times like this, she wondered why she bothered.

Then May had known there was to be no salvation from the moment the Speaker had chosen not to allow a vote on the Andrew Murrison amendment that could have minimised the scale of her defeat. As John Bercow made his ruling, the prime minister's head slumped. There was to be no momentary relief from abject misery. She was stuck in her very public hell.

Geoffrey Cox had tried to cheer her up in his opening speech. The attorney general's last pantomime outing at the dispatch box had attracted mixed reviews and he had received extensive coaching in the interim from the Brian Blessed School of Overacting. But though his technique had improved a little – the voice had a more velvety fruitiness and his arm gestures were more expansive – his material was still desperately thin.

We were where we were. Everything that had taken place since 23 June 2016 had been an ineluctable step towards this vote. The backstop was just an airlock: a holding position between two different barometric states. A nano-second's pause before entering an Albion of hope and dreams. Moreover, expectations of the withdrawal agreement had become wildly inflated. Now was the time for stoical pragmatism. A bad deal was better than a no-deal.

None of this was really true and Cox knew it. As did MPs from both sides of the house who picked him off at will. We were where we were as a result of the prime minister's arbitrary red lines and decision to hold an unnecessary election. On the other side of the airlock was a total vacuum. That expectations had been so high was all of the government's own making. One self-inflicted wound after another.

The more Cox's arguments were dismantled, the more bloated his oratory became. Unable to read his audience, he rattled on for almost exactly an hour allowing himself 10 encores (none of which had been requested). Back at his Devon home, Cox's dog, Lily, put her paws over her eyes. She had warned him there was a huge gap between am-dram and the professional stage but he hadn't listened. He had imagined he was giving his finest Henry V and ended up a cross-gartered Malvolio. Still, she had always preferred comedies.

With Cox having grabbed so much of the limelight, backbench speeches were soon restricted to five minutes. Bad news for Dominic Raab, who had planned on using his as a leadership bid. No one believes in Dom quite as much as Dom does. Or at all. He has a campaign team of one. Dom has even managed to forget he was Brexit secretary when the withdrawal agreement was being negotiated. From here to obscurity.

Thereafter MPs rehashed familiar lines both for and against – mostly against – the withdrawal agreement, while sobbing with tortured self-pity. But no one was listening. They were just waiting to find out what happened next. Come the vote, they were still none the wiser. Except for one thing. Despite a catastrophic defeat, May would survive the no confidence vote. She would remain prime minister. Albeit a prime minister without a clue. A surreal end to a surreal day.

First history, then the hangover: MPs traipse back to the farce

16 JANUARY 2019

The Ship of Fools drifts on, its captain and crew seemingly indifferent to the rocks ahead. There was a time when Westminster was just your average shitshow, but that shark has long since been jumped. A shitshow at least has a certain entertainment value; now there's more fun to be had from having a panic attack. Which is what the rest of the country has moved on to. That and foraging in Jacob Rees-Mogg's recycling for food to stockpile.

And there is nothing average about this parliament. If only. That's a level of elite performance which most MPs can only dream about. It's taken years of training for this bunch just to learn how to get dressed in the morning. Or undressed in Boris Johnson's case. You'd get more sense out of someone who'd overdosed on barbiturates.

Alice hasn't just disappeared through the looking glass. She's kicked in the whole mirror. On the morning after the night before, it was almost as if no one was fully aware of the significance of the government having suffered the most crushing defeat on record.

Rather than a sense of history in the making, there was more a vague sense of embarrassment. As if everyone had blacked out after getting completely trashed and had come round unable to remember precisely what they had said or done. All they had was a lingering sense of having behaved badly. A communal dance of shame in which no one quite dared to look anyone else in the eye.

As ever it was Theresa May who set the tone. At prime minister's questions nothing had changed. The reason her deal had been rejected was because parliament had failed to understand it properly. So as a special treat, she was prepared to sit down with those MPs who agreed with her and explain to them why she was right. And when she had done that she would bring the deal back to the Commons to let them have another go at voting it down.

This wasn't just delusional. It was disturbingly pathological. Jeremy Corbyn tried to introduce a note of reality, but May wasn't having it. At times of crisis her sense of denial inevitably prevails. Those who had spent the morning working on decommissioning her memory had done a decent job. She had already blanked out just how crap she was. She was proud to be the woman without qualities.

Things didn't much improve when the Labour leader opened the no confidence vote. You'd have imagined that Corbyn would have made a bit of an effort with this speech. After all, it was notionally the moment he had aspired to for the past 35 years. He spoke well enough about why May had failed on Brexit, but then even a Question Time audience can manage that these days. He was less than convincing on why he should replace her. Maybe he was just distracted by the knowledge he was certain to lose and would then be nudged closer to a second referendum he didn't want. Or perhaps he was more in touch with the country than he sometimes appears. Most opinion polls have 'don't know' as the runaway favourite to be next prime minister. After the Four Pot Plants.

May defended her record, slowly and robotically. She was a legend: she'd been held in contempt of parliament; she'd lost a budget vote; and now her Brexit deal had suffered a record parliamentary defeat. That was a stunning hat-trick of own goals. And she hadn't even done the decent thing and resigned! Beat that! She was already a YouTube classic. Give her a few more weeks and she'd overtake David Cameron as the country's worst-ever prime minister.

The next few hours were best forgotten as Tories, many of whom had gone out of their way to make plain their lack of confidence in May, went on to say why she had their full confidence and should remain prime minister. Some even wondered out loud why the public had such a low opinion of politicians. They should try listening to themselves sometime. Rebecca Pow sobbed that the Commons should have been talking about Conservative achievements. Not that she could think of many.

Wes Streeting, Stella Creasy and Tom Watson livened things up a bit, but there was no disguising that history was proving to be an anti-climax as no one seriously believed the confidence vote had a prayer. Michael Gove was so sure of victory that, in between rubbishing the idea of Corbyn as a possible prime minister, he took the piss out of May by describing her as 'inspirational' in his closing speech.

Sure enough, the prime minister crept over the line by 52% to 48%; history repeating itself first as tragedy, then as farce. Not that she cared. She had won a vote for the first time in weeks. She was a winner after all.

May made a brief statement finally inviting other party leaders to hear why her red lines still stood. Corbyn and the Scottish National Party's Ian Blackford demanded that a no-deal should be taken off the table: the DUP's Nigel Dodds reminded her she had only survived because of his party's votes and that the price of his continued support was a hard Brexit. And more cash.

The chancellor immediately got out his credit card but May remained impassive. Her face frozen. The Brexit circle could still not be squared and the shutters had gone down again. She wasn't listening. She was barely there. Even in victory, she was a darkness visible.

Boris Johnson digs into the Donald Trump playbook

18 JANUARY 2019

Give it a week, maybe two, and Boris Johnson will deny he ever came to the JCB factory, owned by Brexit-backing billionaire Lord Bamford, in Staffordshire to make yet another comeback speech. That's his current grasp of reality. As a politician he has long since been nothing more than a blond curiosity. A one-man freak show. But as a case study he still has plenty to offer the psychiatric profession. The jury is out. Is he aware he is lying but sees no problem with it? In which case he is a borderline sociopath. Or is he utterly delusional? In which case he is clearly psychotic. Either way, he needs help. Quickly. To save him from himself and to save the country from him.

You'd have thought that Boris had had enough of making leadership bids by now. After all, it's not as if the previous seven or eight have gone particularly well. He is a film franchise dying on his feet. The Return of the Slobbit 9. But apparently not. Boris was back to once again convince the public that the man who had done more than anyone else to divide the country and bring it to its knees was just the person to pull it back from the brink.

Johnson cut to the chase early on. Theresa May's deal was terrible. What she should have been doing was trying to negotiate with the EU which had been all poised to be flexible and drop the Northern Ireland backstop. It made you wonder if he had actually been following the news over the past couple of years. In BorisWorld, Boris the Superhero would go to Brussels, tell Michel Foreigner what's what over a decent déjeuner and get exactly what he wanted. He wasn't saying he ought to be prime minister, but he ought to be prime minister.

Having got Brexit sorted, the Slobbit turned his attention to the reasons why people voted to leave the EU. There was too much inequality. Some people got paid far too much, while others had to make do on next to nothing. Take him as an example. The £230,000 a year he was being paid to write essentially the same article each week – on top of his salary as an MP – was a total disgrace. He should be getting far more than that. No one could survive on £5k a week when they had an expensive divorce to pay for.

Next on the agenda was his record as London mayor. No one had done more to put the capital on the map than him. The cable car that went from nowhere in particular to nowhere in particular was the envy of the world. As was his ability to have £48 million wasted on a garden bridge project that was never going to get built. Not even some of the world's greediest or corrupt politicians would have dared to try to get away with that.

Then to the home straight. A succession of lies. Five Easy Pieces. Brexit would lead to a huge cash boost for the NHS. He loved foreigners. He was a team player. He was doing his bit to keep the Tory party together. A no-deal Brexit would be a no-sweat Brexit. There was a brief pause when the Slobbit reached the finish line as the media briefly considered the possibility that they had been had. That the whole thing had been a wind-up and that Boris was going to break into one of his trademark guilty grins and shout 'Gotcha'.

But he had been serious. As serious as an unserious man with no credibility can hope to be. So the media piled in. Channel 4's Michael Crick challenged him on the remarks that he and Michael Gove had made about Turkish immigration during the 2016 referendum campaign. 'Never said nothing,' Johnson pouted. Crick quoted chapter and verse but still Boris repeated his denials. Just because there was film and written evidence of him doing something didn't make it real.

It was straight out of the Donald Trump playbook. Only sadder and more pathetic. More quintessentially British. A man who can't quite accept that his audience is now limited to his own reflection. In a cracked mirror. And even he can't raise a laugh at his tired one-liners. No one cares any more. He might have been funny once but the world has moved on. All that remains for him is a howling against the dying of the light.

'Is that it?' he said at the end. It was a question everyone had been asking. He disappeared out of sight behind a large yellow digger. The other diggers in the factory raised their arms in salute. They couldn't have dug a better hole for him if they had tried.

* * *

Though many MPs usually welcome the chance to do next to nothing other than repeat themselves, even they have their limits of despair. And a Theresa May statement on 21 January in which she reiterated her determination to pursue a Brexit strategy that had already been voted down by parliament was a step too far for everyone. We'd now reached the point where even the EU had taken to rejecting her latest plans to reopen negotiations before she had got round to announcing them. Because she is that predictable. And that delusional.

Here was the plan. She couldn't possibly rule out a no-deal because that would involve extending article 50. And that was something to which she couldn't agree because that would be tantamount to kicking the can further down the road. This from a prime minister whose only identifiable talent is for kicking cans down the road. As so often, the only person whom the irony escaped was May. Plus ça change. So plan B was the same as plan A. Only with a different font. The UK was well on the road to madness.

After two years of no progress whatsoever, bring on plan C minus

29 JANUARY 2019

What could possibly go wrong? After a series of votes that had decided almost nothing, other than that the House of Commons didn't want a no-deal – though not enough to do anything much about it – and that she should go back to Brussels in search of a deal that wasn't on offer, Theresa May made a short statement.

She was going to phone Michel Barnier – from a withheld number, as the EU's chief negotiator had blocked her Downing Street landline as he was sick to death of having the same, pointless conversation – and if anyone from any other party had anything constructive to add, then she'd go through the motions of listening to them. Workers' rights? Whatever they were, she loved them. And the backstop? Bad, very bad.

Nothing much had changed. We were back to almost where we had been two weeks previously. And two years before that. We were just a bit closer to a no-deal. Through inertia, as much by design. There was no hope. Only a vague sense of futility. Tumbleweed rolling, rolling, rolling. Time passing. The pound falling. Life and reason slipping away.

The prime minister had opened the debate by observing

she had recently consulted widely with members of all parties and come to the conclusion that doing anything to keep the Conservative party together for an extra couple of weeks was more important than the national interest. She was now urging the house to vote down the deal she had insisted only a few days ago was the best Brexit deal that could be possibly negotiated and support instead an amendment instructing her to go back and reopen the withdrawal agreement that the EU had insisted couldn't be reopened.

Even in the by-now familiar Alice in Wonderland world of Schrödinger's Brexit, where everything can simultaneously be and not be, this was a bit of a stretch for many on the opposition benches. Chris Leslie wondered quite how she squared away her claim to be able to secure a deal by ditching the Northern Ireland backstop with her insistence that rejecting the backstop would inevitably end in a no-deal.

This was a category error, as it assumed May's mind followed sophisticated rules of logic. Her algorithms are much more basic: a 1980s Amstrad programmed merely to secure her survival to the end of the day. At which point her memory is erased. Contradicting herself was the least of her concerns.

Here was the deal. She had originally intended for her plan B to be exactly the same as her plan A, but at the last minute it had come to her attention that Kit Malthouse, one of her junior ministers – along with a bit of help from the European Research Group – had done a bit of Brexit moonlighting and come up with a plan C. Or to give it its full name, plan C minus.

So she was now fully signed up to plan C minus that would entail her going back to the EU on a pointless mission to waste a few more weeks and make a no-deal more likely. With that in mind, she was backing the Graham Brady amendment – a simple idea from an extremely simple man – that would instruct her to go back to Brussels and seek some alternative arrangements. She didn't know what these arrangements might be other than they would be alternative. Possibly involving a mixture of grunge and Morris dancing. Either way she was looking forward to losing a negotiation conducted entirely with herself.

This prompted predictable whoops from several of the Brexiters in her own party, with Nigel Evans declaring that Jerry didn't like it up 'em. Nicky Morgan burst into tears. She was suffering from Stockholm Syndrome and had lined up with the ERG because she could no longer tolerate the idea of remaining a backbencher. Just someone love me, she sobbed. Because she can no longer love herself.

After ignoring Yvette Cooper's suggestion that negotiating an entirely new deal before 31 March was a fantasy too far and that an extension to Article 50 was inevitable, May went into her final peroration. She was going to win because she had only been lulling the EU into a false sense of security by bringing back a deal that had been defeated by 230 votes. Now she was going to give it 110%. This time she really, really wanted it. *The X Factor*'s gain was the country's loss. Her new red lines were to get the EU to move their red lines.

In reply, Jeremy Corbyn had little to say. But he was damned if he was going to let anyone else get a word in edgeways, refusing to take interventions from anyone he didn't much like. He has a small friendship group. It was unnecessarily petty and provoked a meltdown on the Tory benches. Cue a near shambles, with dozens of MPs going out of their way to embarrass themselves. Not that they generally need much invitation.

Brexit continues to make fools of all those with whom it comes in contact. Especially those that were already fools. Give it time and most MPs will be only able to speak in non-verbal grunts. A rare win-win. They'd probably make more sense that way. By the close there was almost no one in the house. Had anyone from the EU been bothering to listen in to such a dismal debate, they'd probably conclude they were far better off without us anyway. This is the new UK. Bringing down the average IQ of the whole of Europe.

Donald Tusk's special place in hell looks like where we are right now

6 FEBRUARY 2019

After a Brussels press conference punctuated with know-ing sighs, in which he again made clear the withdrawal agreement was not up for renegotiation but that – as a gesture of goodwill – he was willing to entertain sensible alternative suggestions from the UK government, the EU Council's president concluded with a simple thought. 'I've been wondering,' he mused, 'what that special place in hell looks like, for those who promoted Brexit without even a sketch of a plan how to carry it out safely.'

This was Donald Tusk unplugged. A politician tired of diplomacy that kept going nowhere – 'What bit of backstop doesn't the UK get?' – and happy for once to speak his mind. 'They'll give you a terrible time in the British press for that,' whispered a delighted Leo Varadkar, the Irish taoiseach. Tusk merely smiled. 'Yes, I know. Hahaha.' He no longer cared that much what anyone thought. He had tried to be nice to the Brits but all you got in return was news bulletins with Theresa May in a Spitfire and people comparing the EU's aims with Hitler.

In any case, his question had been largely rhetorical. That special place in hell was only too familiar; it looks pretty much like where we are now. It wasn't one reserved only for an incompetent and negligent elite of Boris Johnson, Michael Gove, Nigel Farage, Theresa May and the rest. Whatever hell they had in mind, they were taking the rest of us with them. Hell wasn't other people, it was the whole lot of us.

A UK where everything was steadily getting a little worse by the day. One where the only hope left was that things might not get quite as bad as everyone feared.

A reality show for self-harmers and the terminally depressed, hosted by Jacob Rees-Mogg. A land of unmanaged decline. The direction of travel was clear. All that remained unanswered was in which circle of hell we were located.

News of Tusk's Dantesque comparison hadn't reached the chamber in time for prime minister's questions, a session that did momentarily stem the slide into the terminal hell of mediocrity. Largely because neither Theresa May nor Jeremy Corbyn were present. The prime minister's trip to Ireland has been a relief to those in Westminster, if not to the Irish.

Instead, the Commons was treated to the two leaders' stand-ins, David Lidington and Emily Thornberry. One of whom can just about answer questions and the other of whom can just about ask them. It makes a huge difference. Not that anyone was much the wiser at the end, as the shadow foreign secretary saved all her six questions for Brexit. Something that no one in government, not even Lidington, who is more clued-up than most, has any solutions for. At least, not ones which they yet dare utter in public. The more Lidington tried to defend the indefensible, the redder he became. It was almost endearing.

Ken Clarke later observed Thornberry and Lidington as being two people struggling to find something to argue over and that it was a pity they weren't actually in charge of their respective parties. Put them in a room for five minutes and they'd come up with a customs union proposal that would be passed with ease by MPs in an afternoon. If only.

The rest of the session passed off fairly uneventfully, with just a couple of Brexiter interventions. Bernard Jenkin wanted to know what was holding up the discredited Malthouse compromise. Lidington's blushes turned a shade deeper. He's so co-dependent he gets embarrassed on Jenkin's behalf. Even though Jenkin is too out of touch to feel it for himself. 'Um,' said Lidington. The reason the Malthouse compromise was going nowhere was because it was basically brainless. Which is why Steve Baker, Marcus Fysh and Owen Paterson had been sent to work on it. Mark Francois just bellowed.

The Tusk fallout only really started when PMQs was over. Andrea Leadsom, one of the cabinet's many useful idiots, was first out of the blocks. She was absolutely devastated. DEVASTATED. She couldn't believe the EU Council president had been so spiteful. We were supposed to be friends, allies and neighbours. It was totally unreasonable for the EU not to completely rewrite its own rulebook for its member states when the UK decided it couldn't agree to something to which it had already agreed. If Brexit ended in tears then it would be the EU's fault. You have to work quite hard to be that dim.

Back in Brussels, Tusk held his head in his hands. What had he done? First all this nonsense, then tomorrow he'd have to lose hours of his life in another meeting with

May. He'd inadvertently tipped himself and the UK closer to the centre of hell.

Commons pummelling leaves Failing Grayling seeing ships

11 FEBRUARY 2019

Earlier in the day the prime minister had once again expressed her full confidence in Chris Grayling. Which left unanswered the question of why. Just how hopeless does the transport secretary have to be for Theresa May to confess that she might just have the slightest doubt about his abilities? Whatever kompromat Grayling holds over her must be devastating.

Grayling is a one-man disaster zone. A figure of such great incompetence is usually only found in cartoons. The only talent Grayling has ever displayed in any of his government jobs is for doing them badly. It's no longer just me who calls him Failing Grayling. Almost everyone does. Including the rest of the cabinet. His reputation now precedes him even in France, where he has been banned from entering the port of Calais. They've got enough troubles of their own en France, merci beaucoup.

It's now also clear that not even Grayling has confidence in Grayling. Long before he was called on to explain the latest saga in the ongoing embarrassment of

Seaborne Freight, his cheek was wobbling uncontrollably with anxiety as he waited on the government front
bench. Soon he will be recognisable only as a Kafkaesque
nervous tic.

'Um, er . . .' Failing Grayling began, his eyes darting
around the chamber searching for someone, somewhere
who might love him. Or if that was too much to ask,
then someone who might take pity on him. Er, he had
always made clear that Seaborne Freight was high risk,
but he had wanted to show that the government was
backing business by handing over a contract to a company that was effectively out of the ferry business. It
was just unfortunate that everything had gone tits up
when some other company called Arklow, which had
said it might help out Seaborne, had done the due diligence his department had failed to do and pulled out of
the deal completely.

As so often, Labour's Andy McDonald was spoiled for
choice in his reply. Being shadow transport secretary to
Grayling is any MP's dream job. All you have to do is
stand up and talk in coherent sentences to be ahead of the
game. McDonald duly obliged by asking whether proper
procurement procedures had been followed, whether
Arklow had signed a contract with Seaborne before the
government had awarded the contract, and how much the
whole fiasco had cost.

'We haven't spent any money,' insisted Grayling.
An answer that didn't entirely square with a recently

published National Audit Office report which concluded that the department had spent £800,000 on consultants and that due diligence had not been done on Seaborne. It can only be a matter of time before Failing Grayling finds himself back in the Commons explaining why he misled parliament.

A few Tory Brexiters gamely tried to defend the transport secretary. But the desperation in their questions merely highlighted the hopelessness of his self-inflicted predicament. Roger Gale got things off to a bad start by labouring under the impression that Seaborne was running an aviation service, so it was unreasonable to expect them to have any boats. He really needn't have bothered.

It got worse. Robert Goodwill and Matthew Offord insisted it was totally unreasonable to expect Seaborne to have any ferries as most airlines didn't own any planes and Uber didn't own any taxis. The fact that they might have access to them – something beyond Seaborne's imagination when it came to ferries – eluded them. It must be a mystery to both of them how anyone ever gets anywhere. Truly, Grayling acts as a stupidity magnet.

Jacob Rees-Mogg detected the sinister hand of Brussels in Grayling's failings. Arklow had sneakily failed to sign a contract with Seaborne just to make a fool of the transport secretary. There was just one fault with this. Why would the Irish company bother to go out of its way to do something Grayling was more than capable of doing on his own? Something he went out of his way to prove by insisting that when the government had originally said it was planning for no-deal, it had only pretended to plan for no-deal as it hadn't thought no-deal was very likely. But when it had become clear that things were worse than they had thought, he had panicked by awarding a contract to Seaborne.

The rest of the session was just a punishment beating for Grayling, with Labour MPs asking for inconvenient details of costs and contractual arrangements. 'I'm doing my best,' sobbed Grayling. 'The minister is handling this as well as possible,' Kevin Brennan conceded. It was just that the bar was pathetically low and the country could do with a transport secretary with basic motor skills.

The SNP MP Drew Hendry tried to break the bad news to Grayling. There were no ships. There never had been any ships. And there weren't going to be any ships

'I do see ships,' Grayling insisted. It's just a shame they were ones that didn't exist. The mystery of his incompetence had been solved. He had been out of his head on acid for years. The whole of Brexit had been one bad trip. Losers in the Sky with Diamonds.

Can you negotiate with people who are certifiable? Ask the EU

14 FEBRUARY 2019

Cometh the hour, cometh the man. And who better to deputise for the prime minister during the latest debate on why the government still doesn't have a clue about what it's doing about Brexit than the Brexit secretary himself? Stephen Barclay's the one member of the cabinet whose job description is to know nothing whatsoever about Brexit. A man put on the payroll for the sole purpose of being kept out of the loop.

In a parallel, fairer world, Barclay would be an anonymous financial adviser, whose only success was to have been runner-up in a lifetime achievement award hosted by the north-east Cambridgeshire regional chamber of commerce for being the only person dim enough to have mis-sold himself his own pension.

Instead he finds himself charged with misleading the country over the government's Brexit policy. A job he does with ease, as he doesn't even know what it is he doesn't know.

Barclay opened the debate by mumbling that it was still government policy not to have a policy. And he was happy to confirm that, as the prime minister had been taken hostage by the European Research Group, the natural consequence of accepting the impossible demands of the Brady amendment calling for the renegotiation of the withdrawal agreement, was that the UK would almost certainly be leaving the EU on 29 March with no deal.

Several Tory Brexiters could scarcely believe their luck. They had been expecting far more of a fight than this and hurriedly sought reassurances that their pre-ferred 'no-deal' was still on the table.

Owen Paterson wanted confirmation that the Malthouse compromise really was as pointless as his appointment to the Alternative Arrangements Working Group had indi-cated. Barclay was delighted to confirm this. He had spoken at length to Jean-Michel Jarre and they had agreed that squads of highly trained, armed badgers were the key to solving the Northern Ireland backstop.

Yvette Cooper asked whether Barclay was still 100% committed to a no-deal even if it meant people losing their jobs or dying. 'Absolutely,' the Brexit secretary beamed. No greater love and all that. Besides, it would only be the weak and the unpatriotic who would be out of work or croak. Those who were prepared to hold their nerve would be absolutely fine.

This didn't go down well with the Tories' Caroline Spelman, who was disappointed to discover that her own amendment that had been passed – expressing parlia-ment's aversion to a no-deal – was not being taken as seriously by the government as the Brady amendment.

Barclay had an answer ready. The only way the

government could send a clear message to the EU showing we were a nation that could be trusted in negotiations was to act in a thoroughly untrustworthy way by cherry picking the best amendments.

Keir Starmer becomes more impressive with each outing at the dispatch box. Mainly because he now merely has to reiterate what everyone, except Barclay, knows – namely that the prime minister was merely running down the clock and, if push came to shove, was quite happy to leave the EU with no deal if that was the price of keeping the Tory party more or less together.

But he is also helped by getting to fend off witless interventions from some Conservatives. James Cleverly tried to claim that May running down the clock was conclusive proof she couldn't be running down the clock, while Alex Chalk didn't even seem to realise he had voted against the government's withdrawal agreement by backing the Brady amendment. This is politics 101. And these are supposed to be two of the Tory party's rising stars.

The one flaw in the shadow Brexit secretary's performance was that Labour had yet to come up with an alternative plan of their own. Every time Starmer produces something vaguely sensible, Jeremy Corbyn puts a red line through it. At this rate, Labour and the Tories are in a race to see which party will split first.

Thereafter the debate followed a predictable course. It was the same as every other Brexit debate, only a bit more rubbish. The more serious the situation becomes the more it resembles a third-rate farce.

The only thing that comes close to uniting the Brexiters and Remainers is a mutual distrust of anything said by the government front bench. The idea that a minister might actually be able to distinguish between truth and lies – or even achieve something – has become unimaginable.

It ended in chaos. First Anna Soubry pulled her amendment as the government had indicated it would provide an impact analysis of a no-deal Brexit. Then both the Leaver and Remainer Tories abstained so that the government was defeated on the main motion it had won two weeks previously.

You couldn't make it up. May could not even win a meaningless vote. Which, ironically, in itself had meaning. Humiliation. For her and the country. The EU must be pissing themselves. How can you negotiate with people who are certifiable?

Corbyn immediately demanded that May go to the dispatch box to give a statement declaring she accepted that her strategy had failed and that she would come back with a plan that could win a majority in parliament. Which would have been a start.

Only there was no sign of the prime minister. And none of her ministers was prepared to take the hit for her. Only the sound of a clock ticking to break the silence. May was holed up in Downing Street. Her software stripped bare. Searching for a programme. Any programme. Control. Alt. Delete.

Inside Labour's lonely hearts club band

18 FEBRUARY 2019

It was always going to be a race to see which party split first. And when push came to shove it was Labour that beat the Tories to it. Monday morning during half-term week in the etc. venue of London's County Hall might not be everyone's idea of a good time to launch a new party. The Etc. Declaration doesn't have quite the same ring as the SDP's Limehouse Declaration of 1981. Despite this, the airless, corporate fourth-floor meeting room was rammed half an hour before the new Labour breakaway supergroup appeared.

On stage were seven empty orange-brown, leather-ette chairs, a high stool and a lectern with a blank sheet of paper covering the new logo. We now had an idea of how many were in the band, but just who they were and who was going to be Val Doonican and get the stool no one knew. There could not have been more excitement if Steps or S Club 7 had said they were making a comeback tour. With 10 minutes to go, the new party's name was revealed to be the 'Independent Group'. Catchy.

As the clock ticked well past the 10am starting time, there were rumours of splits in the split before they had split, but then a voice called out: 'They're coming down the corridor.' Elvis was in the building. Moments later, several bouncers cleared the aisle and the expected figures of Luciana Berger, Chris Leslie, Angela Smith, Gavin Shuker, Mike Gapes, Ann Coffey and Chuka Umunna made their way to the stage and headed for the seven seats.

Berger took the first solo and rather fluffed her lines by introducing herself as a Labour MP. She appeared close to tears as she hastily corrected herself. Enough was enough. She was embarrassed and ashamed by the institutional antisemitism that the leadership had wilfully failed to address. She had had enough of bullying, bigotry and intimidation and had now resigned to stand as an independent MP.

For the next key-change, Leslie was on lead vocals. Breaking up was hard to do, he confessed. But it had been Labour that had changed, not him. He was still committed to the same values on which he had first been elected. The party had betrayed its supporters over Brexit and he could no longer remain while Corbyn was in charge. He was also sure there were many other MPs who secretly felt the same way and he hoped the Independent Group might be able to collaborate in the studio and do gigs together at a later date.

The other five solo slots pretty much reprised the first two. A bit of country and western personal backstory, a reiteration that it was others, not them, who were to blame for their artistic fallout with the Labour party and a shout out to others to join them. The main differences were in tone. Coffey and Smith adopted the minor key of regret, Gapes went for full-on anger while Umunna opted for the sensible, pragmatic approach. Shuker was rather hampered by the fact he was largely unknown, so had to explain who he was and why he had been invited along as a backing singer.

Things began to unravel slightly when the new band were asked to explain what they were for rather than what they were against. It had been so traumatic for all of them to leave the Labour party after so many years of trying to get their voices heard from within, that they had forgotten they were supposed to have a new album and tour to promote. This was the launch that failed to declare what it was exactly that was being launched.

No, they definitely weren't a new party. They were a movement. Though they might become a party at some point in the future. Just don't hassle us, man. They didn't even have a leader. Though it was possible that Gary Barlow might take over at some point if his recording schedule allowed.

No, they weren't standing down to trigger by-elections as that wasn't what their fans would want. No, they weren't going to form an alliance with the Lib Dems as the Lib Dem brand was toxic, but if any Lib Dems wanted to join them that would be OK. And they would quite like some left-of-centre Tories to join them, too, though so far those MPs were still in a contract dispute with their record labels.

And that was that. Seven Labour MPs who had been openly at odds with their party had now decided to go it alone. It felt less a major political realignment than a cry of regret and irreconcilable despair. No one could quite work out what they had done or what they had achieved. If anything. Not even them. And we never did get to find out who the stool was for.

Labour and Tories, for once, were a lot closer than they like to think

20 FEBRUARY 2019

It was Britain at its most British. In any other country, the sight of 11 MPs – eight from Labour and three from the Tories – taking their seats next to the DUP on the opposition benches for the first time as the Independent Group (TIG) for prime minister's questions might have caused a stir. Or even a comment. Instead everyone was determined to keep any embarrassment to a minimum. Don't mention the war, don't mention the war.

Both Theresa May and Jeremy Corbyn restricted their exchanges entirely to Brexit. As a non-aggression pact rather than a serious line of inquiry. On any other day, Brexit might have been awkward for the two party leaders – it hardly counts as a specialist subject for either of them – but now it was more of a pleasant fireside chat.

Anything to keep away from the main issue of Labour and the Tories haemorrhaging MPs.

Not that we actually learned anything new about Brexit – other than the prime minister still didn't have a clue what she was doing and was staking her career, what was left of it, on Geoffrey Cox doing the decent thing and giving a guarded thumbs up to whatever non-legally, legally binding fudge she could come up with in the next week.

How was it all going, Corbyn asked. Oh you know, May replied. As well as could be expected. Nice weather we've been having. That was the interrogation at its most incisive. Thereafter, both leaders danced on eggshells. Corbyn was so set on maintaining a polite atmosphere that he even found himself praising the record of the Blair-Brown government. Something he's never knowingly done before. He's going to hate himself when he watches a video replay of his performance. Much more of this and he could even split from himself. An unconscious uncoupling.

The closest anyone came to mentioning that which could not be mentioned was when Conservative Maria Caulfield raised the case of a Labour councillor who had defected to the Tories. 'Yes, yes,' May said brusquely. This was the big split on everyone's lips. Now could we please not bring it up again? The omertà was intact. Even the 11 TIG MPs felt bound by it. None tried to ask a question and instead just chatted happily among themselves. PMQs was just symptomatic of a broken politics, man.

One day they might get round to asking May what her favourite colour was, but for now they would rebel in silence. Anarchy in the UK. I mean it, man.

Heidi Allen, Sarah Wollaston and Anna Soubry were more talkative at a press conference shortly after PMQs to announce their defection. There were rather fewer hacks at this one than had been at the Labour do on Monday – seen one split, seen them all – but the breakaway 11 almost became the breakaway 10 when one of the chairs collapsed as they were surrounded by photographers. Fortunately no great damage was done and once the debris had been cleared, Allen stood up to speak.

The Labour S Club 7 event had been a funereal affair, with each MP in turn using their five-minute slot to share their experience, strength and despair in a group therapy session for rough-sleeping politicians. Allen was determined to put the party back into the party that was not yet willing to call itself a party. She was a woman reborn. She had been delusional ever to join the Conservatives, as she couldn't think of one good thing they had ever done. Now she was her own person, the real Heidi. She could dare to dream. Her *X Factor* pitch was oddly uplifting.

Wollaston was more measured – delivering her terminal diagnosis on the state of the Tory party with the solemnity you would expect of a doctor – while Soubry just went for it. Few MPs give better rants than her.

The Conservatives had been taken over by anti-EU zealots from top to toe. People like her – and there were many others thinking of jumping ship, she insisted – had been utterly marginalised as the ERG had taken the prime minister hostage. Enough was enough. The revolution started here. And it would be televised.

Soubry was less convincing when she recalled memories of the halcyon days of David Cameron. Not even the shed-bound Dave is that deluded. Then again he has yet to reach the point in his memoirs where he became prime minister, imposed austerity and split the country with a referendum that only a handful of his own MPs wanted. Writer's block. He's stuck in the bromance of the Rose Garden.

Cometh the hour, cometh Geoffrey Cox's wobbly codpiece

7 MARCH 2019

You had to admire the sang-froid. Just 24 hours after returning from the Brexit negotiations in Brussels where he'd spent the entire working dinner being asked: 'Are you having a laugh?' and 'What planet are you on?' in a variety of European languages, Geoffrey Cox was back in the Commons looking entirely unruffled to face attorney general questions. Top lawyers have to get used to winning and losing. The secret is being able to dress up the losses as successes. Something at which Cox is a dab hand.

If Cox was bewildered that the EU had proved resistant to his baritone – normally he only has to open his mouth to have people eating out of his hand – he didn't show it. Rather he settled straight into his familiar patter. He was only here to serve. Though sadly, it broke his heart to say this, that he was bound by legal convention to be unhelpful.

But he was committed – he dabbed away a tear at this point – to giving the house what it needed. In so far as he could. For now, all he could say was that it was a shame Johnny Foreigner had so far been disobliging. Not to have been offered even the smallest sweetener was the very height of rudeness. The sort of thing that had caused major wars in the past. Cox took a deep breath. Duty called. Noblesse oblige. So he would return to Brussels shortly to continue discussions.

Challenged by Labour's Helen Goodman to say whether he was still trying to reopen the withdrawal agreement or just hoping to get some minor form of soothing words that might allow him to revise his legal opinion on the binding nature of the Northern Ireland backstop, Cox was indignant. 'It's come to be called "Cox's Codpiece",' he said, to nervous laughter. 'What I am concerned to ensure is that what's inside the codpiece is in full working order.' Brexit reduced to a series of knob jokes.

This didn't entirely answer the question. Were the contents of the codpiece too small to be seen except under a microscope? Or were they largely a load of balls? The SNP's Patrick Grady was far from convinced, observing that as the attorney general wasn't going to be able to change a word of the withdrawal agreement there didn't appear to be much hope of Theresa May's Brexit deal getting voted through second time round.

The plans for the vote were not his to decide, Cox declared loftily. But as far as he was concerned the proposals he had been discussing were careful and coherent. As clear as day. He just couldn't understand why the EU were being so wilfully unreasonable. It was perfectly obvious that if the UK was not prepared to break its own red lines then the EU would have to abandon theirs. What could be more straightforward than that?

These were difficult times, he conceded. But cometh the hour, cometh the Cox. And he was happy to lead his country in its time of peril. He very much hoped he would one day soon be in a position to change his legal opinion to the government's advantage, but that time had not yet come. But if it did, he would pleased to come back to the house to update it. He sounded like a barrister who was expecting his client to get a long prison sentence.

Brexiter Mark Francois still wasn't happy. Then he never is. Neither was the shadow solicitor general, Nick Thomas-Symonds. Given the attorney general was now leading the negotiations and would then be pronouncing on their legal implications, wasn't this the equivalent of marking his own homework? 'The law is the law,' he boomed. And besides he could see which way the wind was blowing. Brexit was such a shambles that a

Chilcot-style enquiry was sure to follow, and he wasn't about to sacrifice his reputation just to get the prime minister's second-rate deal over the line. No matter how much she begged.

Still the questions came in. Labour's Hilary Benn, chair of the Brexit select committee, tried to discover whether the government was also proposing to change the existing arbitration mechanisms for the backstop. 'Ah!', Cox nodded. That was entirely dependent on what question one wanted to ask of the arbitration mechanism, because the question asked might very well determine if the protocol was effective. Everyone looked blank. It was the kind of non-answer lawyers are paid a fortune to give.

After briefly lamenting the stupidity of cabinet colleagues Karen Bradley and Chris Grayling – he would leave them to their own legal scrapes – Cox brought the proceedings to a close. He once more regretted he was legally bound to be unhelpful, but if it were to emerge that he could be helpful in a way that was also helpful to him then he might break with legal convention. We'd all just have to wait and see. Cox sighed. This pro bono work for the government might be good for the soul, but it was a lot more trouble than it was worth. Note to self. Don't answer the phone the next time the prime minister rings.

This was May unplugged, unvoiced and once more exposed

12 MARCH 2019

Things fall apart. It was a victory of sorts. But Theresa May was in no mood to celebrate seeing her Brexit withdrawal agreement being defeated by a mere 149 votes compared with 230 first time round. This was a second humiliation even she could not ignore. Rejected by all the opposition parties. Rejected by 75 of her own MPs. Rejected by herself.

Not that she didn't try. In her statement after the defeat, the prime minister insisted her deal was still the only deal on offer. It was bordering on clinical madness. Her limitations as leader once more exposed. This was May unplugged. Unvoiced even. Her words no more than the occasional gasp.

Even when she glimpsed reality by barking out that there would be a no-deal vote the next day, she was unable to prevent herself from more self-harm by declaring she would fail to whip it. Weakness piled on weakness. The martyrdom of St Theresa. Condemned by her own hand. A kinder Tory party would put an end to her suffering right now.

Things fall apart. After her late night trip to Strasbourg, May had briefly dared to hope her revised deal might just have a chance. That lasted as long as it took for the attorney general to deliver his verdict. Many had thought that Geoffrey Cox could be persuaded to finesse his way to giving the prime minister a free pass on the legal status of the UK's right to withdraw from the Northern Ireland backstop. Instead the country's top lawyer turned out to be more interested in his integrity than acting in his party's interest. It was a dangerous precedent for an attorney general.

The man with the golden voice looked haunted as he explained his decision to the Commons. Having a conscience clearly came at a price. It was like this: the previous week he had travelled to Brussels to negotiate a new deal. And it was only when he was then asked to mark his own exam paper that he realised he had actually failed.

Things fall apart. But there were failures and failures, Cox explained. His was a failure with merit. One that deserved at least a hearing to explain the magnitude of his failure. For to concentrate purely on the legal aspects of the legal status on which he had been asked to provide an opinion was a category error. Or to give it its proper title, Bollocks. What parliament had to understand was that the legal difficulties presented by the backstop were a secondary issue to the political expediency of getting a bad deal passed.

Parliament isn't used to hearing a lawyer telling it not to bother about the law and after a brief pause – more of a reality check – dozens of MPs began openly laughing at Cox. The attorney general looked hurt. His was not a comedy, it was a tragedy – one that deepened with every intervention. Having to spell out the UK would be subject to the European Court of Justice in any arbitration procedure was pretty much the final straw. He exited stage left, an honourable if chastened man.

Things fall apart. Moments later, May entered the chamber, glanced up at her husband in the gallery and gave a resigned shrug. She knew the game was up already, with both the Democratic Unionist Party and the European Research Group having already declared their opposition to her deal.

The Tories also looked as if they knew they were in the endgame. Though the front benches were padded out with a few cabinet members rounded up under duress, the back-benches were at least half empty for what was meant to be one of the most important debates in the country's history. There's only so much pain anyone can take.

Things fall apart. The prime minister got up to speak but all that came out was a barely audible croak. Just as at the 2017 Conservative party conference, her voice had its own narcissistic, psychosomatic breakdown. A total malfunction brought on both by stress and a limited awareness she was the architect of her own misfortune. The Maybot was now in the process of decommissioning herself. She wanted to speak, but her voice knew she had nothing to say.

It was almost too painful to watch. A prime minister with an unerring self-destructive instinct for making the wrong call, trying to win over a group of hardcore

Brexiters, red-faced and blue-blazered, whose one mission appeared to be to prevent Brexit. As if it had only ever been the longing and sense of grievance that gave them meaning. In winning lay only emptiness: a sense of existential futility. Pathos and irony locked in a death spiral.

Some words did escape her lips, but few were heard. The odd loyal Tory backbencher did offer half-hearted support, but most either kept silent or stayed away. Even the Four Pot Plants covered their leaves in shame. That bad. It felt like the end of days. A government out of ideas and all but out of power.

Things fall apart. Seventeen days and counting. A government, a parliament, a country with no direction. Sans eyes, sans teeth, sans everything.

As the losses take their toll, May is now a leader in name only

13 MARCH 2019

First as tragedy. Then as farce. Finally as sheer batshit craziness. Even by her own standards, this was a new low. The prime minister cannot now even win what should have been a gimme, something with which she fundamentally agrees. Having resorted to whipping against the motion she had championed the day before, after her attempts to get the Caroline Spelman amendment pulled had failed, she now found herself on losing territory again. On current form you would back Theresa May to come second in a one-horse race.

The losses are taking their toll. As she rose to explain her latest defeat, it became clear an arm had fallen off. A manically rotating eyeball was dangling out of its socket. Her voice still no more than a hollow, metallic rasp. The sound of a 1980s computer testing the beta version of a language script. Possibly English.

She had listened to the house, she croaked. This was a lie, a programme error. Her entire career has been based on never listening to anyone. She is the Maybot, coded on a stubborn, solipsistic loop. She has only ever heard what she wants to hear: the voices in her head.

She had listened and basically she had won. Her deal was still the best deal, even though it had been twice voted down by Brexiters more consumed by self-harm and self-loathing than delivering Brexit.

May is now a Leader In Name Only. LINO. Too weak even to sack ministers who abstained or voted against her three-line whip. The Commons has descended into near anarchy, a Wild West with every man and woman for themselves. Particularly on the Tory benches, where party loyalty has almost completely broken down. So much so that virtually every vote is now in effect a free vote.

Even cabinet unity is a distant memory. Something Philip Hammond made no attempt to conceal during his spring statement. Normally these occasions are red-letter days in parliament, but with the general level of clusterfuckery at Defcon 1 this was a total non-event. Ordinarily the chancellor puts only his audience to sleep: today he almost managed to get himself to nod off as well while announcing the important acquisition of a new computer in Edinburgh.

Then Hammond went rogue. Who cared if LINO was sitting next to him? She didn't count anyway. It was time to level with the country. The statement was a waste of time. He couldn't say what was going to happen in the next two weeks, let alone make a stab at what might happen in six months' time.

If we left the EU with a deal then we'd all be a bit more broke than we otherwise would have been. But if we left with no deal then we were totally screwed. Might as well give up and kill ourselves. So LINO could shove her deal. Now was the time for the government to work with the opposition on what might get through parliament. His door was open. With her one remaining functioning eye, LINO gave her former colleague a death stare – an effort that caused her circuit board to crash entirely.

With the woman who couldn't listen now transformed into the woman who couldn't move – let alone speak – it was left to Michael Gove to open the debate on taking no-deal off the table for the government. Not exactly the ideal man for a crisis, as he is not someone given either to self-doubt or conscience. He is the almost complete political sociopath, someone who invariably finds that his principles bend to his own advantage. Most people wouldn't trust him with their Nectar card, let alone a government department. In recent weeks he has gone out of his way to keep as low a profile as possible while the shit hit the fan. Just in case the fan were to hit the shit.

The environment minister began by paying tribute to the prime minister. She was a brilliant, brilliant woman who had never put a foot wrong. This was the kind of eulogy that invariably precedes an assassination, and sure enough Gove went on to use the next hour as his audition for the top job.

First he went out of his way to distance himself from any responsibility for the current situation – no, no, no, he'd never told any porkies during the Vote Leave campaign – and then he tried to reassure MPs that though it was the government's default position to leave with no deal, leaving with no deal was the last thing he and anyone else in government wanted. Even when he's trying to be sincere, he just sounds glib. A Poundland playground populist. Then he went for the big pitch. He too was open to offers of cross-party indicative votes. So forget Hammond, ring him instead. The LINO was an ex-LINO. His self-regard was almost total. Whether he believed a word he said was anyone's guess.

Keir Starmer, Yvette Cooper, Jess Phillips and Dominic Grieve all spoke with passion and clarity, but some of the rest of the debate was taken over by the idiocracy. While Crispin Blunt and John Baron insisted that all the businesses in their own constituencies wanted was the certainty of going bust on 29 March, Iain Duncan Smith and Steve Baker pushed the fantasy of the Malthouse compromise that had already been ruled out by the EU. Give it time and they will gradually get to 2019.

In his winding-up speech, Liam Fox sounded so deranged it sounded as if he was going to vote against the motion for which he was notionally speaking in favour. No deal. No surrender. Remember the Faroe Island deal. Mad. Even by his standards.

Then came the vote. Things fall apart. Again. The entire country reduced to a third-rate reality freak show. An international laughing stock. Anarchy in the UK. We mean it, man!

Day 993 in the Big Brexit House, and another crank of the pathos handle

14 MARCH 2019

Finally. Theresa May had found a vote she could win. A narrow two-vote victory. A largely pyrrhic victory, as the government had won on a motion to extend article 50 it had never actually wanted to put to the house in the first place. Even when the Leader In Name Only is winning, she still contrives to lose. Another crank of the pathos handle. The government still just about had control of the parliamentary timetable. For a few more days at least.

Not that LINO took any pleasure in the result. No smile escaped her lips, no signifier of relief. Just a hunched figure, lost in a near catatonic state. She clearly hates her life almost as much as she hates many of her colleagues. Hating is one of the few things she does well. The body language between her and Philip Hammond was of a couple who had long since realised there had never been two of them in this relationship. She left long before the final result was declared.

With LINO's voice on either life support or a damage limitation exercise – take your pick – it had been left to the Cabinet Office minister, David Lidington, to open the latest Brexit debate the government had been hoping to avoid. He looked like a man who knew he had drawn the short straw.

Lidington is usually one of the cabinet's more able performers. He knows his brief and, unlike many of his replicant colleagues whose mere presence makes the flesh crawl, he has a basic humanity and integrity to which even opposition MPs readily respond. Yet he too has been corroded by Brexit. Not so much in his fundamental honesty, but in his self-doubt.

His self-confidence is shot, anxiety is now lined in his face and he has developed a nervous tic. Not as pronounced as Chris Grayling's, but similar. Perhaps it's contagious, the inevitable legacy of spending too much time close to ministers who don't know what they are doing and have no authority. A government whose only doctrine is to fail. Fail again. Fail better. Samuel Beckett's time has come.

Lidington hopped from side to side nervously, like someone who had mistakenly imagined that only 12 double espressos could get him through his impending ordeal. He began by trying to lay out the government's position. A near impossible task when it changes by the hour. If LINO was in any position to enforce this, then we'd now have reached the point where ministers could face show trials for thought crimes for failing to understand that she no longer believed what she had believed in the morning.

Um, er ... As far as he knew, what the government currently thought was that if the Brexit deal was passed then the UK would ask for a short extension to the article 50 process. And if it wasn't then we would have to ask for a longer one. Which wouldn't be good as we might have to spend £16 million on European elections. Rather less than Failing Grayling manages to waste in an average morning.

Predictably there were countless interventions, with MPs quick to observe they were being asked to forget the government had previously said it would never ask for an extension because it would never be granted and it was only the prime minister's own incompetence that had led to this current request – which now apparently would be granted. Hilary Benn and Oliver Letwin both made the very obvious case that it was clearly time for parliament to start thinking about what it did want. Lidington didn't seem to think that a good idea at all.

Other contributions were rather less illuminating. Tory Edward Leigh wondered if the best way out of the backstop might be to rip up all our treaties and declare war on Brussels. Mark Francois announced that he'd just been to the gents and wanted to know if anything had happened that he'd missed. There was. The last five years. One feels for his next of kin.

The uncertainty was catching. Keir Starmer has generally been playing a blinder, but he too now looked like someone operating on a faulty autopilot. Partly through fatigue, but mostly because he was being asked to defend the indefensible. If it was hard enough trying to convince the house it could get a completely new deal agreed with the EU inside three months, it was a near impossibility to sound convincing when he said that yesterday would have been a good day for a second referendum, tomorrow would be a good day for a second referendum, but today wasn't. He sat down, his head bowed with embarrassment. A bad day at the office.

Day 993 in the Big Brexit House. The inmates had voted for something, but nobody was quite sure what. We were now well into an infinitesimally small 12th dimension. A near airless vacuum, devoid of intelligent life. Somehow all but 15 Tories, along with six Labour Leavers, had managed to convince themselves that they didn't need to take back the control they had once voted to take back. They were happy to be guided by a prime minister who clearly didn't know what she was doing. No one knew anything. Least of all LINO. In the final vote, the Brexit secretary, Stephen Barclay, who had summed up the debate for the government, turned out to vote against the government. The cabinet now has a collective death wish. A parliament of donkeys led by nematodes. The country went to bed praying there would be no tomorrow. Where's an asteroid when you need one?

Ziggy Bercow and the MPs from Mars rock old hit Erskine May

18 MARCH 2019

Days like these, Theresa May must wonder why she bothers. A question many of us have been asking for a couple of years. If she wasn't in enough trouble with the hardliners of the European Research Group, Conservative Remainers and a Democratic Unionist Party hot on the scent of more cash, she now had her namesake on her back: Erskine May. Or at least the Speaker's interpretation of the parliamentary rulebook.

Shortly after 3.30pm on what had hitherto promised to be a quiet afternoon in the Commons, John Bercow decided to give the government his own kicking. Like most things the Speaker does, it was delivered with much theatricality and self-importance but was none the less deadly for it. Having previously ruled that some precedents were made to be broken, he had concluded that the precedent of not allowing a government to put the same – or substantially the same – motion to the house as one that had previously been rejected should be upheld. So if the prime minister wanted to put her Brexit deal to a third meaningful vote, she was going to have to come up with something radically different.

Labour MPs, who have always suspected the Speaker was a not-so-secret Remainer, were effusive in their praise. He had put a stop to parliament being strong-armed, bullied and bribed. He was a saint. A latter-day people's hero. The man who hadn't just sold the world, but had also saved it. Ziggy Bercow. The Speaker puffed up with pride. It wasn't for him to agree that he was as marvellous as everyone said, but if others wanted to make that assertion who was he to gainsay them?

It was Hilary Benn who asked the killer question: could the Speaker confirm that a substantive change would have to be one agreed with the EU and not some dodgy deal cooked up with the DUP on the back of an envelope? Bercow was more than happy to do so. Anything to make life as difficult for the prime minister as possible.

Brexiters also appeared quite pleased with this result, bizarrely reckoning it made a no-deal exit more likely.

Quite how they reached this conclusion was anyone's guess. Logic has never been their strong suit. Tory MP Mark Francois checked to see if this also meant a second vote on a second referendum was now also off the cards. Ah, said Bercow. That didn't follow at all. Context and circumstance was everything. And that would be interpreted however he happened to feel on the day. But don't hold your breath.

Having been given no notice of the Speaker's statement, the government front benches were all but empty with only Amber Rudd, who had been taking work and pensions questions, from the cabinet in situ. She looked like a woman who had just realised someone had thrown up all over her, making it clear that responding on behalf of the government was massively above her pay grade and dashing for the exit as soon as indecently possible.

Eventually the chief whip, Julian Smith, and Andrea Leadsom, the leader of the house, filed in. Smith rose to make an intervention then thought better of it. There was probably no point in doing his primal scream therapy in public. Leadsom kept her head down, avoiding the Speaker's eye while punching texts into her mobile.

But the hotline to the Leader In Name Only (LINO) was only lukewarm. No 10 had no more clue about what was really going on than anyone else. The text exchange merely read:

Leadsom: WTF?

LINO: WTAF?

Leadsom: WTAFF?

LINO: WTFAFF?

The only time Leadsom spoke was to say she wouldn't be talking to the Speaker unless he was a lot nicer to her. There is no love lost between the two. We've reached a stage where almost everyone hates everyone else.

With no guidance from the front bench, a few Tory loyalists tried to ad lib. James Cleverly suggested that it would have been more helpful if Bercow had made the ruling between the first and second meaningful vote, so that all those MPs who had wanted to waste everyone's time before coming on board could have had the chance to do so last week. Cleverly is living proof of the fallibility of nominative determinism. Matthew Offord just said it was all a bit unfair. A bit how his constituents must feel having him as their MP.

This was a whole new level of Brexit clusterfuckery. The previous week's chaos now merely looked like one of the more unfeasible *Matrix* plotlines. Just with no Keanu Reeves. A room full of chimps could make a better fist of things. Some MPs talked of proroguing parliament; others of a general election – with 11 days to go till 29 March. Hey, at least it's still double figures.

For LINO it was just one more humiliation. Not only would she be going back to Brussels to ask for changes to the withdrawal agreement she wasn't going to get. She would now be asking for an extension on a deal she was now unable and too scared to put to a vote. Not even the Four Pot Plants can help her now. But on the plus side, at least we're giving the rest of the world a good laugh. The UK: not just a reality freak show, but also a feel-good movie. We fail so they don't have to. It's a legacy of sorts for the government.

Pity poor Barnier, a man in search of the UK's plan

19 MARCH 2019

Michel Barnier looked troubled. He'd always worked on the assumption it was the EU that took negotiations down to the wire, but now it was the UK that was taking the piss. We weren't into injury time so much as injury time to injury time. A liberty even Alex Ferguson wouldn't have demanded of a referee.

At a press conference to mark the end of a general affairs meeting at which he had been keeping foreign ministers up to speed, the EU's chief negotiator tried to make sense of the situation by talking himself through the current state of play.

A withdrawal agreement had been agreed between the EU and the UK. The only one possible given Theresa May's red lines. That much he knew for certain. After that it all got a bit confusing as the UK parliament kept rejecting it. Not that it was too much peau off his nez.

The EU was more or less ready for no-deal if that was the way the UK wanted to play it, but if the prime minister was going to ask for an extension, she first needed to get a bend on and then tell everyone why she wanted one. Asking for an extension merely because you need a little more time to work out why you want an extension was not going to cut it.

What Barnier really wanted to hear was some kind of plan. A sense of purpose. His reality checker then cut in, as he remembered it was the Leader In Name Only he was dealing with. Someone whose only discernible talent was her indecision. He quickly lowered his sights. Maybe a sense of direction was asking too much. He'd settle for a few hints expressed through interpretive dance. Not waving but drowning. Let's keep things simple, he said. After all, this was the UK. A country that appeared to have nominated itself as this year's comedy nul-points entry for the Eurovision Song Contest.

Here was the deal reduced to its basics: the UK could ask for a short extension or a long extension. But it couldn't have both at the same time. The Schrödinger options of the short extension that could simultaneously be long or the long extension that could also be short were both non-starters. Quantum contradictions may be the current foundation of UK politics, but the EU preferred to stick to the Newtonian model. Compared with his British counterparts, Barnier was a model of clarity. An adult politician delivering an adult message. There would be no freedom of movement of the UK clusterfuckery to Brussels, merci beaucoup.

Back in the UK, LINO was making some progress. She had finally noticed that the government was in crisis. Better late than never. But not, apparently, at such a late stage of crisis that she actually needed to come to a decision. Because after a long cabinet meeting at which precisely nothing had been agreed – things have now reached peak inertia, with ministers no longer either able to remember exactly what it was they had promised to resign over or even if they had any principles in the first place – the only clarity was that there was no clarity. How do you ask for an extension that you promised everyone you would never ask for?

LINO knew she was due to write a letter to Donald Tusk but, after several hours sitting at her desk, she had got no further than Cher David. Aidez-moi s'il vous plaît. Je suis completely out of mon depth and have no idea what I wanter. Other than to crawl under a rock and hide for the next few jours. Je am un hostage de la Conservative party. Best wishes, Theresa. PS Can you getter moi a EU passport?

With the UK effectively in a state of limbo – why panic when there were still 10 days in which to do nothing? – the only vague signs of leadership were to be found on *Good Morning Britain*, where Piers Morgan sharp-elbowed his way into Susanna Reid's interview with Tony Blair. The country's future momentarily in the hands of the two most disliked men in the UK. Blair looked gaunt and, even when he was saying something reasonable, couldn't help but appear shifty. Morgan, meanwhile, has turned himself into a one-man Alan Partridge tribute act, a narcissist of modest intelligence who has no idea that he is actually the joke. Much like the current government. Onwards and sideways.

* * *

Just seven days before the UK was officially due to leave the EU, Theresa May dashed back to Brussels to hijack a summit meeting that had originally been scheduled to discuss trade with China, to ask for an extension to Article 50 if she failed to get her deal though parliament. It didn't go well.

At last May manages to unite both the country and the Commons

22 MARCH 2019

For any other person, the EU Council meeting would have been shit or bust. But given that Theresa May has long since treated the last-chance saloon as a drop-in centre for the soon-to-be homeless, we are now well beyond that. The Leader In Name Only has taken herself to the realms of shit and bust. A space-time continuum where she has failed upwards and upwards to the point where there are no good solutions on offer in any imagined universe. She is the kamikaze pilot doomed to crash her plane into the sea over and over again for all eternity.

LINO had started the day in reasonably good spirits. For once, she had managed to unite the whole country. The TUC and the CBI had released a joint statement saying she was useless. Both Labour and Tory MPs had been so thoroughly pissed off by her Bob Geldof 'Give me your fucking votes' telethon appeal that they were even more likely to reject her deal than they had been before she had opened her mouth. Every one of her cabinet ministers was plotting to get rid of her. No one anywhere had a good word to say about her. In an act of misplaced martyrdom, LINO had brought a nation together. If this was her being on their side, they'd hate to see what she could do when she was against them.

Having left Gavin 'Private Pike' Williamson in charge of activating the nuclear bunker under No 10 – on reflection, not the safest pair of hands for an apocalypse but needs must – LINO had headed off to Brussels for her latest final showdown. On arrival, she had appeared characteristically shifty when she was asked by reporters what she was going to say to the EU. Plan? Why were people expecting her to have a plan? That was the kind of question her cabinet kept asking her. She hopped nervously from one foot to the other, telling the cameras she was determined to be determined before beetling off mid-sentence.

That turned out to be pretty much a rehearsal for her meeting with the 27 EU leaders. A punishment beating for all concerned in which LINO managed to talk for 90 minutes but say almost nothing. Five minutes with May has been enough to have most people screaming for heavy medication. Munch had had it easy. Time and again, LINO was asked what she would do if she failed to get her deal through at the third attempt and each time she stared at the floor. The sound of one brain cell desperately seeking out another. It's the closest to human contact she gets these days.

Evasion and deceit are now hot-wired into her basic circuitry. LINO can no longer remember what she has said to whom. Or even if it matters. No self left to be divided. In January she had told parliament the UK hadn't voted for a no-deal Brexit. Now it was her default option. Last week she had promised to seek a long extension. Now she had her heart set on a short one. Her battery life is near zero. Words, language and meaning have all collapsed in on each other. Everything is nothing. She is now almost inchoate. Her existence reduced to minute-by-minute survival. Am I alive? Am I still prime minister? The rest is silence.

As so often, LINO's inability to articulate her basic needs – food, water, deal, no deal, death – left the EU in a state of thinly disguised fury and their discussions stretched well past the point where both the double act of Jean-Claude Juncker and Donald Tusk and May were supposed to give their press conferences on what had or hadn't been agreed. Shortly before midnight, white smoke emerged. A deal had been offered that LINO was obliged to take. Her 90 minutes of tough talking to the EU had resulted in an offer considerably less than she had demanded. She has a way with words. Juncker and Tusk merely looked like indulgent parents who had prevented a crisis for a few more weeks at least. And would do so again if necessary. Whatever it took for the UK parliament to get its act together. Until the very end of time.

Twenty minutes later, LINO blinked her way into a brightly lit upstair room to give a press conference of her own. She appeared to have taken part in slightly different negotiations. For her the main sticking point had been getting the EU to agree to the Stormont Lock that no one had been talking about and would infuriate the ERG. As for the extension, 22 May and 12 April were pretty much the same as 30 June.

Besides, she was still going to get her deal through parliament because parliament would bloody well do what she wanted though obviously she respected the views of MPs who disagree with her. Everything in her body language suggested the opposite. She just can't do contrition. Asked what she would do if her deal was voted down, LINO retreated into a random series of zeros that could mean anything and nothing. It was a strange, semi-detached performance of a prime minister struggling to convince herself she was still in charge.

Bonjour tristesse. Taking back control had come down to handing back control to the only grownups left in the room. A woman and a country humiliated both by a refusal to accept reality and by the thrilling rush of self-harm. Whether her deal eventually went through or not, her time was up. She had broken herself and her party. And in the process she had taken the country down with her.

Theresa May's global comedy TV show is a big hit in Europe

22 MARCH 2019

Well, that went well. Theresa May: Her Part in Her Downfall. Episode 1,002. Having used her traditional hardball negotiating skills to come away with an offer she had never wanted, the Leader In Name Only scampered back to the UK at the earliest possible moment. So it's just as well we're not hoping to sign any major free-trade deals with China in the near future. Sod you China, we've got the Faeroes in the bag.

Before the latest Brexit clusterfuck caused everyone to drop everything, the main item on the agenda of this week's European Council had been the negotiations to hold negotiations about a trade deal between the EU and

China. A huge delegation of Chinese officials and journalists had descended on Brussels for the occasion and they weren't best pleased to be sidelined to a one-hour slot on Friday morning. Nor were they impressed that LINO hadn't bothered to stick around to apologise for messing them about. Remember that time when LINO said the UK would play a full part in the EU until the day we left? She doesn't. But China will.

Apart from among the Chinese, there was a genuinely bearable lightness of being in the air inside the Council of Ministers once May had gone. Her greatest gift to the EU is her absence. The relief in her departure is much the same as you get when a migraine finally wears off. Or when Question Time finishes. Most European leaders would rather have surgery without anaesthetic than spend another hour in her company. She is the singularity of infinite density at the heart of a gigantic black hole.

With LINO back in Blighty, the EU was free to indulge in what has become its favourite pastime. Trolling the UK. Our gift to the world is to offer hope to failed states and provide amusement to all other countries. Brexit has never been about sovereignty or taking back control. It's been setting ourselves up as a global comedy TV show franchise acted by a cast of the grotesque and the inadequate. For years to come, Dave will be broadcasting repeats on an endless loop. In between finishing his memoirs.

It was the French president who sounded most pleased to see the back of the prime minister. When she had begun her 90-minute piece of self-destructive absurdist performance art, Emmanuel Macron had rated her chances of getting her deal through the British parliament as no more than 10%. By the time she had finished, he had revised that down to 5%. Donald Tusk, the European Council president, reckoned that was being generous. Whatever hand she held, she could be relied on to play it badly.

Après Macron, le déluge. At a side meeting of European Economic Area and European Free Trade Association countries, Iceland declared it wouldn't be at all happy having the UK as a member. We were just too much trouble. We'd try to change the rules before we'd even joined, refuse to meet our obligations and then demand to leave. Nobody would ever get anything useful done. The EEA and EFTA would be in permanent gridlock. Existing merely to exist. The bottom line was that the UK was too Poundland for Iceland.

Things weren't going any better back in the House of Commons, where Labour took advantage of a rare Friday sitting to ask the Brexit secretary for his take on how the European Council had gone. As Stephen Barclay's sole job is to know almost nothing about anything, he conveniently made himself absent and left Kwasi Kwarteng, the most junior member of the department, whose sole job is to know less than the cleaners about what is going on, to take the hit.

It was a bloodbath from the off. Not only is Kwarteng a round peg in a round stupidity hole, no one in government had actually got round to considering that some kind of plan might be needed after the EU had taken back control the night before. So he was left to make things up as he went along, while MPs on both sides of the house openly mocked him for his incompetence. He must have done something hideous in a previous life to deserve his current one.

Kwarteng's basic line was that some things might probably happen, but if they didn't then some other things, as yet unspecified, might happen instead. He couldn't be any clearer than that. As the laughter around him grew – several MPs shouted 'Is that it?' – Kwarteng panicked and began to make up government policy on the hoof. Indicative votes, meaningful votes, free votes. Everything was both on and off the table.

How could anyone tell if he was telling the truth, or even agreed with what he had said five minutes earlier, Kwarteng was asked. They couldn't, he replied confidently. But if no one else was going to come up with something that resembled a plan then he might as well do it himself. Cometh the hour, cometh the Forrest Gump. Ecce homo!

Over in Downing Street, things were just as bad. LINO had holed herself up in her bedroom and was refusing to come out. She shouted at the mirror that she had really nailed it in Brussels. She was a winner. 'It's over,' her reflection said, shaking its head not unkindly. 'Enough is enough.' Then it gradually dissolved until May was just staring at nothing. Now she really was completely alone.

Brexit Westminster is like *The Crystal Maze* on crystal meth

27 MARCH 2019

The only person missing was Prince Edward. Brexit has now turned Westminster into *The Crystal Maze* on crystal meth. A looking-glass world where any truth has a half-life measured in milliseconds, where normal rules no longer apply and every MP is desperate to play the joker. The best the rest of us can hope for is to wake up to find we had been dropped into the ninth series of *Dallas* and that the last few years have just been a bad dream. Imagine how good that would feel.

This was the day when the pupils chose to put their own school in special measures because they had lost faith in their teachers. When parliament sought to take back control of parliament. Precisely the form of taking back control the government had always insisted the country didn't have in mind when it had voted to take back control. But then the government now barely has control over its bowels as everything it touches turns to shit. There is no area of public life it hasn't found a way to do badly.

First though, we went through the formalities of prime minister's questions. A formality not just because Theresa May is Leader In Name Only but because Oliver Letwin was the de facto prime minister for the day. For LINO, it seemed like something of a release.

Now that even she seems to have realised she has reached the endgame of her time in office, she appeared almost demob happy, in as much as someone whose automated language skills barely extend to meaningful sentences can do. She still insisted she had no intention of listening to anyone but herself, but made no effort to deny her sell-by date was near. The last sign of artificial intelligence in a Maybot is an awareness of inbuilt obsolescence.

The school's new timetable didn't get off to the most promising of starts. After Letwin had apologetically read out the lessons for the day – he does everything apologetically, even on rare occasions like this when he has nothing to apologise for – Jacob Rees-Mogg merely used the time to debate the merits of different public schools. The UK's biggest constitutional crisis reduced to a spat between Eton and Winchester over Tudor history. Beyond pathos.

The Grand Wizard of Mogg has always resembled a boy in a suit. Now he's just a homunculus trapped inside a boy's body, mewling at the moon to distract everyone from his own sense of entitled inadequacy and profound misjudgment, and unable to even own that it was partly down to him that the government had temporarily lost control of Commons' business. If nanny had been around, he'd have been sent to the naughty step. For life.

LINO wasn't quite done, however. There was still time for another unnecessary act of self-harm as she whipped her party to vote down the business of the house that had been agreed only two days previously. She punched the air as she crashed to yet another defeat. Losing has become an obsessive compulsive disorder. Failure is her defining feature, the only thing at which she indisputably excels. With any luck, she'd lose again providing John Bercow didn't stop her from bringing the meaningful vote for a third time and the Democratic Unionist Party didn't do something stupid like saying it would vote for her deal after all.

But LINO needed back-up, a get-out clause. So she headed off to the 1922 Committee to deliver the coup de grâce, the sacrificial self-immolation. She knew she was useless, she told the Tory backbenchers. She had always been hopeless. And now was the time for everyone to acknowledge they too thought she was rubbish by getting behind her deal that they all thought was terrible. If they did that, she'd promise to resign sometime over the summer. She wasn't entirely clear on dates, but then she's seldom clear on anything. All she cared about was that she'd created the ultimate lose-lose situation, both for herself and the country. She would go down in history as the worst ever prime minister. So far. The ideal outcome.

Boris Johnson tried to look sombre as he left the 1922 Committee but he couldn't conceal a smirk. Everything was working out just fine. Who cared if the public reckoned him to be a man of no principles? He'd never pretended to be anything but a self-interested careerist. Brexit had only ever been a means to an end. He could live with vassalage if necessary. Having blown it once back in 2016, he now had another shot at the top job. His face crumpled just a little as he belatedly realised he'd be struggling for support among fellow Tory MPs who did have scruples. Hopefully, there wouldn't be too many of them. And a little Latin would impress the rest.

What followed was yet more clusterfuckery. The ERG split, the splitters split from the splitters and then the hardcore Spartans threatened to bulldoze parliament in the name of democracy. Just before 9pm the shit really hit the fan when the DUP found there was no deal to which they could say yes. No retreat, baby, no surrender. LINO's deal was as good as dead and she'd made the ultimate futile gesture.

As so often we ended up by knowing less than when we had started. Friday had been cleared for a third meaningful vote but no one knew if it would now even take place. Just how much more of a punishment beating was LINO willing to take. She couldn't even organise her own departure. The only upside was the distress on Boris's face. His venality had been all in vain. The pneumatic huckster had just slashed his own spare tyres.

The quantum Brexit had become ever more relative. And parliament was still left wondering quite what it had taken back control of as it had contrived to vote against everything. Bollocks to everything. The will of the people was to remain indefinitely in a tenth circle of hell. We were supposed to be leaving the EU in two days' time. Time for the Four Pot Plants.

Everything is up for grabs in Schrödinger's Brexit

29 MARCH 2019

On the bright side, Theresa May got her margin of defeat down into the high double figures. But long before the votes were counted, the Leader In Name Only knew the game was up. Waiting to make the closing speech, her eyes were vacant, her body shrunken. She was a shell, all but absent in both mind and body. The black hole of Brexit had almost totally consumed her.

LINO wasn't battling for her political life. That effectively ended when she announced her planned resignation earlier in the week. But when it came down to it, she didn't even have the self-worth to fight for her self-respect. Her appeals to party and country were half-hearted at best. A mere going through the motions of someone whose final act of sacrifice was comprehensively rejected. It was never a choice between her or her deal. It was both. The ultimate humiliation.

The hardline Brexiters were as good as their word. There was no Brexit they could vote for. Bill Cash, Steve Baker, Owen Paterson and John Redwood had been very clear about that. They had devoted their lives to fighting those bastard Johnny Foreigners in Brussels and they weren't going to let Brexit stop them. Imagine a life with nothing to moan about; nothing to get out of bed for. Without the EU, life was a meaningless void. They were the parasites who couldn't survive without their host.

Once the result was declared, LINO stood up to give her losing statement. She's getting so good at them that she hadn't even bothered to write a winning one this time. Her voice was no more than a dull monotone. The Maybot on life support. Once again her language function didn't even run to binary.

She knew she had lost, but that was about it. She didn't have a vision because she never had. LINO was right out of ideas. She'd see what happened during the second round of indicative votes and then do something else. Probably bring back more or less the same deal that had now been voted down three times. When in doubt, crash yourself and revert to default settings. Besides, one more defeat wouldn't be so bad. Brexit had got her hooked on failure.

Even Geoffrey Cox sounded flat when he opened the debate. His usual ringing baritone was flattened around the edges. A once great actor was now no more than an end-of-the-pier tribute act; a diminished ham playing to near empty houses. And no one knew better than the attorney general that the part he'd been given was a dud.

Trying to separate the withdrawal agreement from the political declaration was never likely to fool anyone. Especially, the Labour Leavers whom Cox was sent out to woo. Why would anyone trust a government that had repeatedly proved itself to be untrustworthy and which would soon have a leader whom they trusted even less than the last one?

The rest of the five-hour debate was mostly a refrain of all the others. After nearly three years, most MPs have long since said everything they had to say about Brexit. Like LINO, they too are now on repeat. The one exception was Dominic Raab, who stood up to say that you would still need to be insane to support an exit deal as bad as the one the government had negotiated. But because he now realised he was clinically certifiable, he was going to vote for it. It was the first time anyone had ever launched a leadership bid by effectively ending it. His last remaining cohort of Spartans who would never take yes for an answer would never trust him again. A small win on the day.

This was the day when Big Ben was supposed to ring at 11pm to mark the UK's departure from the EU. When the Red (white and blue) Arrows did a fly past. When new 50p coins were worth 40p. Instead, we were back in a looking-glass world where everyone knew less than they did before. It can't be long before no one knows anything. Back to the future.

Everything was up for grabs in Schrödinger's Brexit: when we were leaving, if we were leaving and how we were leaving; who would be the prime minister, and if there would be a general election. Anything and everything was still possible. Parliament had said something but no one could interpret the language it was speaking. A delegation of ministers was going to No 10 to speak to LINO, but there was no guarantee she would be there. She is lost even unto herself.

There was just one certainty. By voting with the government, Boris Johnson had traded his principles for his career. But then we had always known he would. Johnson's untrustworthiness is the only solid thing the country has left to hang on to. A Newtonian rock in a Quantum Brexit. We really are that far up shit creek.

May has kicked her Brexit can firmly into Corbyn's face

2 APRIL 2019

Almost three years into the Brexit process and trust levels are near zero. After a seven-hour meeting, the cabinet had been frisked for their phones – Oi Gove, I want your burner as well – and kettled inside No 10 to prevent them from blabbing. This was one statement that Theresa May would get to make that the country hadn't already heard from someone else.

Timed to coincide with the six o'clock news, the Leader In Name Only walked nervously towards the Downing Street lectern. Understandably, as the last televised speech she had given from there had pretty much alienated every MP, along with the entire country. This time she kept it short and sweet. A crisp three minutes. But true to form, even at that length no one was entirely sure just what she had said. Or what it meant. Or if it was even possible.

LINO began by all but ruling out a no-deal Brexit. Though leaving the back door open just a smidgeon to one. She was fed up with bashing her head against the DUP and the Spartans of the European Research Group, so now she was going to try her luck with Jeremy Corbyn. Having kicked the can down the road for months on end in a desperate effort to keep her party together, she was now kicking it firmly into the Labour leader's face. There was one question Jezza had to ask himself: 'Do I feel lucky? Well, do ya punk?'

What she hadn't said was what compromises she was prepared to make. Mainly because she simply didn't have a clue. You don't get to resolve a lifetime of indecision in one cathartic, blinding moment of clarity. A Maybot is, as a Maybot does. The only real conclusion her near-obsolete binary brain had reached was that Brexit was a complete mess and, if at all possible, she didn't want to go down in history as the prime minister who had deliberately chosen to tip the UK into recession and civil unrest.

Mostly she was just fed up, though. If the entire country was stressed out by Brexit, how did they think she was feeling? Just imagine what it must be like to be the person in charge who didn't have a clue. She had felt so alone. Especially with a cabinet full of idiots. So it was time to let someone else have a go. And why not Corbyn? He'd been going on enough about how he had all the answers, so let him put up or shut up.

May was also sick and tired of the Tory party tearing itself apart. Hell, there was fuck all left of it to fight over now anyway. Most of her MPs and cabinet were barely on speaking terms with each other now. Some of them were barely even on speaking terms with themselves, they had changed positions so often. They were an anarchic rabble. She might be LINO but the Conservatives were a Party In Name Only. She'd be gone soon and there would be nothing left for her successor to lead. With any luck. Pick the bones out of that, Boris.

So why not have some fun in her last few days and see if she could get the Labour party to tear itself apart as well? Let Corbyn feel the heat for a change. Was he going to insist on a second referendum or would he settle just for a customs union and single market? Were Labour basically a party of Remain or Leave?

Either way, it was no skin off her nose. If the cross-party talks fell apart – as they probably would – and the decision came down to a series of binding indicative votes with her deal as one of the options, she could live with that. All that really mattered was that she shouldn't get the blame. The one thing she had learned from getting up close and personal to a shitshow was that it was always better to have as many people as possible with their arms, elbow-deep, bathed in shit. After all, it wasn't as if there wasn't more than enough of the stuff to go round. The Grand Wizard of Mogg and Mark Francois made sure of that.

As she walked off camera, LINO breathed a sigh of relief. Things would unravel. Of course they would. Even if Labour did play ball, something would go wrong with the extension or the European elections. That was the whole point of Brexit. Things fall apart. The centre cannot not hold. There was literally nothing on which enough people could agree. But she had come out of the day alive and had bought herself the best part of a week. And given how the day had started, that was cause in itself for celebration.

Brexiters castigate PM for denying them what they voted against

3 APRIL 2019

You wait weeks for one prime minister to come along and then five turn up at the same time. On Tuesday night,

Theresa May gave up the unequal battle. She'd already tried offering her resignation but her backbenchers had hated her so much they had kept her on life support by voting down her deal a third time. So the Leader In Name Only of the Party In Name Only had taken the nuclear option and invited Jeremy Corbyn into Downing Street for a couple of days' work experience.

All of which turned prime minister's questions into something more like prime ministers' chats. Both prime ministers had walked into the chamber at roughly the same time and their exchanges began with an unfamiliar courtesy. Corbyn thanked LINO very much for the hospital pass and LINO replied that she would be delighted if he accepted her offer of taking responsibility for her clusterfuckery of the past three years. A level of politeness only possible between two people who disliked each other intensely.

As they were going to spend most of the afternoon arguing over who was going to sit in the biggest chair in No 10 – 'After you.' 'No, after you.' 'But I insist.' – the Labour leader thought it only proper to steer clear of Brexit for PMCs. Rather he just treated it as a desultory dry run for a general election – not that he really needed one now as he was already in power – by asking about poverty.

LINO had shrugged dismally and said she was doing her best but it wasn't easy when you were part of a non-existent government whose sole purpose was to do as little as possible. On the grounds that everything it did try to do invariably turned into a complete shitshow. She muttered something about universal credit and how she hoped she would have a decent retirement when the PINO finally got bored with their sadism. Corbyn's reminder that she would now have to pay for her TV licence when she reached 75 almost broke her. It's always the little things that tip you over the edge.

'Let's talk about what's happening under a Conservative government,' she said. Let's not, murmured everyone on her own benches. Why keep bringing up the war? LINO had entered the Commons to near silence from her own benches. Not even her cabinet can now look her in the eye. Her authority, if you could ever have called it that, was completely shot. She had never been loved – it's hard to feel an attachment to the inanimate – but there had been a grudging respect for her resilience. Now there was just undisguised hatred. The Brexiters would never forgive her for denying them the Brexit they had voted against.

The biggest cheer from the Tory ranks came when Nigel 'Who he?' Adams, who had resigned as a junior Wales minister earlier in the day, was called by the Speaker. Adams bristled with passive-aggression as he kept Brexit to an implied subtext and asked about disabled facilities in Selby station. LINO looked helpless. She didn't even have the power to organise the installation of a lift.

Après Adams, le déluge. What followed was an almost constant blue-on-blue action as Tory after Tory called her out on Brexit. How dare she betray the one true Brexit?

How could she even consider roping in the Labour leader to the negotiations? He was a red bouncing on the Downing Street bed. An antisemite. A scourge of everyone in the home counties.

Under the constant onslaught, LINO cracked and defaulted to her Maybot factory settings. Yes Corbyn was a threat to national security, she barked. And that was precisely why she was inviting him to resolve a national emergency. It was quite bonkers. She had openly insulted the man she was looking on to bail her out of a crisis before any talks had got under way. Her capacity to self-destruct is almost limitless. Everything turns to dust in her hands. Naught's had, all's spent. What little chance of the two prime ministers ever agreeing on a Brexit deal had been strangled at birth.

With Corbyn and LINO off to talk through their irreconcilable differences with their divorce lawyers, three other apprentice prime ministers – Oliver Letwin, Yvette Cooper and Hilary Benn – tried to fill the vacuum. But with only partial success. Benn's amendment to force the Commons to have further indicative votes next Monday was defeated. When push came to shove, parliament couldn't even decide on whether to decide – to agree whether to agree – with the votes tied on 310 and the Speaker giving his casting vote for the government. The first time this had happened since 1993. That was over Europe too.

The second vote on the main Cooper motion to have a debate on making the government seek an extension in the event of a no-deal Brexit sneaked through by 312 to 311. There would be a debate but whether MPs would be able to agree on the meaning of parliament taking back control for a third time was anyone's guess. The government was horrified at the thought of MPs rushing through legislation. If they could just chill out and wait for the government to fail to do anything, the whole process would be redundant. As so often, we had ended the day knowing less than we had started. Still, at least two of the five prime ministers were still standing. For the time being.

Pleeze Sir Graham Brady Sir, can we have anuvver go to get rid of the prime minister?

8 APRIL 2019

Dear Sir Graham Brady Sir,

I am wrITing to you in a perSONal capacity as the aNGRiest member of parlyment. I am very very very AnGry with Theresa May. Or in her case, TheRESa Maybenot, if you Get my drift. It has come to my attenshun that when we had a no confidence vote last DeCember many of uz were not in possession of all the facts.

So it was not a truly deMCRratic vote like the 2016 referendum wuz. Back Then we knew everythink about wot we were doing and 17.4 million heroically voted to be poorer in a no deal Brexit so that GREAT!! Britain never never shall be slaves to the hated eU. So now we want anuvver go to get rid of the prime minister pleeze. Nothing less than the future of our beloved Country rests on you saying YES.

We are livining in a world GONe mad. One where idiots Like me get to go on TV loads and loads. So it's not all bad. But sUM things are very very bad and there is nothing worse than a Conservative prime minister – Propped Up by a Ssinister Remainiaciacal caBBAL in the caBINet – trying to keep us locked into a dreaded CUS-Toms unION foreffer.

That wOUld mean under EU law I would never be able to change my name bak to Mark Frank. At least that's what Andrew BridGIng told me and he knos everyFink. And hes my Frend so there. So THank God, who is ENG-LISH through and THREw, for the unelected Lords for standing up against the democratically elected House of ComMUns and trying to keep No Deal on the table. Or TABle as the fRench call it.

And wot you Might Ask are all the so-called Brexiteers in the govenmint doing? I'll tell you what they are DOing. Absolutely bloody nothing. They are just sitting around on their Fat Arses eating pizza with prOSHooto topping. Typical. They can't even order in a proper British Pizza with ham and pineapple. PatriotISMism is going to the dogs. So since the 'OFFFicer Class' has let us down so badly, it's left to the Poor Bloody Infantry to lead the fightback. Private MArc Francis of the UninteLLigents Corp reporting for DUTY sir, Sir Graham Brady Sir.

Which brings me on to my Next Point. It is an outrage to every normal red-FACed Englishman that the prime minister is actively CONSorting with a known Marxist. The loyal Spartins of the EUropean Reseach Group did not nobly vote down Theresa MayHEM's – see what I did vere? – deal to take us out of the dreaded EU three times only for hur to cosy up with Jereyours CorBIN a man who has been on holiday to Cuba and eats more than his fair share of vegEATables in order to take us out of the dreaded EU.

And another FINg. That letter the prime minister Rote to the EU Council about the extenTION. Total fuckin liberty, if you'll excuse my languidge, Mr Sir Graham Brady Sir. I'm just at the end of my tether. I reeLLY am. First she hopes to fool parlyment wiv a bill that is so long that most orDINErry MPs wont be able to read it proply. Then she only GOES and commits us to taking part in European elections that might even turn out to be a total waste of time as we MIte have left and lets hope they are as if THEres one thing worse than fighting European eleCTions it's having MEPs. It's a totul shambles.

I would also like to remind you I was once Junior Europe Monitor in the school cadet force. A TOUR of DUTY in which I was happy to serve with exTINction. What I learned dURing that time was the EU doesn't like it up em. So it's time for us to stop being such COW-ARDS. We need to tell Johnny Forriner where to get off and then he will cave in and tell us to sod off without a deal. sPeshully if we as a Conservtive party have given the prime minister the push on the wEndsday afternoon before she TAKES her begging bowl to Brussils.

The future of the WHOLE Country is now in the hands of just 313 Conservative MPs. If we get this Write, we happy few can reright the course of history and make our Country a failed state and the LAUGHING stock it deserves to be. But only you Sir, Sir Graham Brady Sir Sir, can make this Happen. So I am bEGGing you, begging you on my hands and Nees – no mean feet as I'm not sure if I'll be able to get back up again – to rethink. In the nAME of God, give us a second vote. Democracy demands NO less.

Yours ever,

Mark Francois. And you can shove the cedilla where the son dont shine.

* * *

After her deal had been defeated for a third time, Theresa May announced that she would now be opening talks with the opposition parties in a bid to find an agreement that could pass in the Commons. Some might argue that if she had done this two years earlier, she could have saved herself a lot of pain and got her deal through with Labour votes. That, though, would have involved compromise.

Not the prime minister's strong point. Brexit had always been more about maintaining the fragile unity of the Conservative party than the national interest. Jeremy Corbyn and the Labour front bench were torn by May's approach. While they didn't want to do anything that would make it look as if they were actively obstructing a deal, nor did they want to make life easy for the Tories when there was a possibility the government might fall and a general election in the offing.

There was also the tricky problem for Labour that it couldn't agree exactly on what it wanted. Some were insisting that a second referendum, to allow the country to vote on whether the final deal was what it had had in mind when it had voted to leave the EU, should be a pre-condition for any deal. Others were happy to settle for membership of the customs union. Or a customs union. It was never clear which. Or what the difference between the 'a' and 'the' really signified. Luckily for Labour, May proved as intransigent as ever. Her idea of consulting with other parties consisted of them telling her what they wanted and her doing exactly the same as she had before. So after a two-week period in which not much happened, the talks inevitably collapsed. May then had to head back to Brussels to request a further extension to the extension she had already been given.

May malfunctions on arrival in Brussels and lapses into old script

11 APRIL 2019

Action and . . . smile. Many people had been bewildered when a shaky, hand-held video of an almost human Theresa May had appeared on the Sunday news bulletins. Especially as she had had nothing to say. What they hadn't realised was that it was a dress rehearsal. All part of a Downing Street plan to get the prime minister to appear, if not chatty – her carers weren't miracle workers – then at least not language obsolete before her emergency Brussels summit.

Her confused, semi-detached ramblings at the last meeting of the EU Council had seriously pissed off the other 27 leaders, who in turn had chosen to humiliate her by sending her off to sit in a side room on her own for hours on end. Without even a takeaway pizza menu. This time there must be no repetition. The upgrade was in place.

On the plane to Belgium, the Leader In Name Only had felt good. At prime minister's questions, Jeremy Corbyn had asked her nothing difficult about Brexit, choosing instead to focus on the forthcoming local elections. And as she had already been told the Conservatives were likely to be wiped out, there had been no real harm in her failing to give any answers. Sure she hadn't exactly covered herself in glory as the Labour leader chalked up an easy win, but you had to take your blessings where you find them. Besides it was hard to pretend you were running the country when it was clear to everyone that it was Yvette Cooper, the Labour party and the EU who were calling the shots.

As LINO got out of the car and prepared to take the red carpet walk past the media into the EU Council building, she felt her nerve fail. 'You can do it,' her carers told her, doing their best to sound encouraging. But she couldn't. The moment she saw the cameras, she froze and went straight to Maybot. Her mouth opened unnaturally wide in what she hoped would be mistaken for a fixed grin and her eyes rotated wildly, refusing to fix on any one object.

She was here to ask for an extension to 30 June, she insisted, accidentally lapsing into the script of two weeks previously. But still she ploughed on. Yes, she might have had that request turned down the last time she was in Brussels, but there was no harm in having another bash. Maybe the other 27 EU leaders would either forget that they'd already said no or realise they'd made a hideous mistake.

After that it was all downhill. LINO gabbled something about the possibility of a hypothetical longer extension that would never be needed because she was still determined to get a deal agreed by 22 May anyway. All the preparations for the UK taking part in the

European elections were just an exercise in nostalgia. A last chance to savour the build-up to printing MEP ballot sheets and booking voting stations before we closed the door on Europe forever.

Everyone looked on amazed. This was delusional even by her own standards. What bit of there being no majority for her deal – or any other deal for that matter – did she not understand? LINO was undeterred. Her systems went rogue and the binary code began writing itself. She was looking forward to a brighter future. When was she looking forward to it? Some time at the end of May. Not her, the month. Or was it the other way round? She lapsed into silence and was led away.

Moments later Emmanuel Macron stepped on the red carpet. He had admired Donald Tusk's style in openly calling for EU leaders not to humiliate the British prime minister as they had last time. And the time before that. There was nothing more humiliating for May than having an open letter instructing people not to humiliate her. So the French president chose to dig the knife in a little by reminding the UK that it was effectively on an ASBO and there would be severe penalties if it misbehaved again. The rest of the EU had very important business to attend to and it wasn't going to tolerate being messed around by a failed state. So he'd make her sweat a bit.

Not that there was much need for that, as LINO was already in a state by the time she began her presentation to the EU leaders. It wasn't her incompetence that did for her. Hell, she'd got used to that by now. It was the look of pity on the faces of everyone in the room that broke her. Each and every one of them saw her for what she was. A leader stripped bare, reduced to little more than a museum curiosity. Merkel tried to break the ice by showing her a cat video on her iPad. Nothing doing.

'So what would you actually do with a long extension?' LINO was asked. She shrugged. Now she came to think of it, she really didn't know. She wanted an extension because she wanted an extension and having an extension was better than not having an extension. That was about it. Oh, and having an extension would enable her to carry on as LINO for longer, as she'd only promised to go once a deal had been reached. Just imagine, a rolling extension to a rolling extension. She could be useless indefinitely.

It took until long after midnight before anyone could begin to make sense of what LINO had said. She has that effect on people. Most countries were happy to give up the unequal and agree to the never-ending extension, but Macron wanted to hold out a punishment beating. The UK had asked for a 30 June deadline that it didn't want and he was going to give it a 30 June deadline he didn't want. The classic Brexit lose-lose.

With eyelids closing and everyone reaching for the cyanide, a compromise was reached on a Halloween deadline that suited no one. And Macron was allowed to save face by putting the UK on the naughty step with a performance review in June. If our MEPs were behaving badly in the European parliament, then we were going to get a very public telling off and the whole world would laugh at us. Even more than they were already.

LINO was too tired to care. Not that she had a choice. The UK had long since ceased to have a meaningful say in anything. It was the EU that had taken back control. Now she could go back home and do nothing again. Another walking holiday in Wales perhaps. Everyone could down tools till the end of October. At which point the shit would hit the fan all over again.

After Donald Tusk had used his press conference to openly troll the UK – hell, there had to be a payoff for staying up so late – it was a rather beaten up British prime minister who appeared before the British media to give her version of events. Her voice was halting, staccato. Almost as if she was trying to fight back tears. There's only so often anyone can spin another defeat as victory without an existential cost.

Things had gone entirely to plan, she pleaded. There was still a chance we could avoid the European elections and leave within weeks. All that was needed was a whole herd of pigs to fly. None of this had been her fault. The blame lay entirely with everyone who had made her prime minister. There was no need to ask her what she would be dressing up as for Halloween. She would be coming as herself. The living dead. If that didn't terrify the EU into giving us another extension, nothing would.

Nigel Farage pledges to deliver UK into promised land of bankruptcy

12 APRIL 2019

To lose one official before your party has even been launched may be regarded as a misfortune, to lose two looks like carelessness. Last month, Catherine Blaiklok, the designated leader of Nigel Farage's new Brexit party, was forced to stand down for making Islamophobic comments and retweeting a neo-Nazi. Then the treasurer, Michael McGough, who quit after antisemitic tweets he posted were uncovered. Say what you like, but you can't accuse the Brexit party of not offering equal opportunities in racism.

At the party's official launch, at a metal finishing factory under the M6 on the outskirts of Coventry, a tanned and disturbingly healthy-looking Nigel Farage was keen to let bygones be bygones as he basked in his coronation as leader.

'No more Mr Nice Guy,' Farage declared. No great revelation, as there never had been one. Nige had just been minding his own business, hoovering up cash on the far-right chat show circuit in the US, appearing alongside racist conspiracy theorists, when his country came calling. 'Oh, I couldn't possibly, but if you insist.' Brexit was being betrayed by politicians, business and – er, the trade unions – and he was the saviour who was going to deliver the UK into the promised land of bankruptcy. His messiah complex is quite strong.

This was to be a new start, a time for the British people to rise up against the career politicians. Said the career politician, who had been bankrolled by Brussels as an MEP for 20 years, had tried and failed to get elected seven times to Westminster and was now heading up his second political party. Farage has never been one to let a spot of cognitive dissonance get in the way of the enjoyment of his self-image. Neither have his supporters. The collective delusion of Nigel as a man who gives a toss about the people has worked just fine for them all.

The British people were lions being led by donkeys. What the country was crying out for was a snake-oil chancer who had just dropped into the bookies to put £1,000 on the Brexit party winning the most seats in the May European elections. People should just sit back, vote for him and enjoy the ride. He had no policies because, well, policies were the sort of thing that establishment career politicians cared about. He was here to offer a dream. A dream of a nostalgic return to the 1950s, when Britain was still just about hanging on to its empire. The independence of a failed state.

But this wasn't all about Nigel. Not entirely, anyway. Having lapped up the attention and the applause of the 100 or so people in the audience – if there was no crowd he still couldn't be entirely certain if he really existed – Farage promised to introduce us to the stellar candidates who would be representing the Brexit party in the May elections. Candidates whose qualities would far exceed those of all their rivals from the political elites.

Step forward the shiniest star, Annunziata Rees-Mogg. To be fair, she doesn't quite have the affected Edwardian upper-class tones of her brother, Jacob, but her posh country accent doesn't really mark her out as a woman to set her disaffected people free. 'I come in sadness,' she insisted, though she actually sounded rather chipper about her trip to the Midlands. Like Nigel and Jacob, she too is a career politician who can't resist any passing microphone. She's just a failed career politician, having been unable to get elected to Westminster even when handed a very winnable seat in the West Country by the Conservatives.

Nancy, as David Cameron liked to call her, turned out to not have much to say, either. But then the Brexit party isn't actually for anything, other than to channel a sense of frustration. If they were ever called on to deliver on the fantasies of a no-deal Brexit, Farage and Stigmata would be the first out the door in horror. You wouldn't see them for dust. Still, Nigel was right about something. The underwhelming Rees-Mogg was slightly more impressive than the other prospective candidates, one of whom was adamant that British fish wanted to be eaten by British people and ripped up her prepared speech in protest at her own mediocrity.

The presentations over, Farage took centre-stage again for a few questions. How was Brexit any different from UKIP? Nigel put on his sincere face. While it was true that they basically shared the same policies – as in they didn't have any – UKIP had turned out to be a racist organisation. And he was having none of that. Oh no. Anything he might have said about immigration in the past, including the openly racist poster of the referendum campaign, had merely been aberrations.

He was a changed man. Someone who just wanted to do the best for his country. None of this was about him. He hated having to be dragged back into the limelight. But duty called. Believe that and you'll believe anything.

* * *

Early May saw yet more own goals from the government. First Chris Grayling had to admit that cancelling all the Department of Transport's no-deal ferry contracts – because the UK, er, hadn't actually left the EU – had cost the taxpayer £50 million. His department having to pay out an extra £33 million to Eurotunnel for being in breach of procurement rules hadn't helped either. Then defence secretary Gavin Williamson had been sacked for allegedly leaking details of a National Security Council meeting on the awarding of 5G contracts to Huawei.

In the meantime, preparations for the European elections, in which the UK was obliged to participate as we had not left the EU, were well under way. The Brexit party, which had not even existed just weeks earlier, was surging in the polls. As were the Lib Dems with their strong 'revoke Article 50' message. The newly formed Change UK were flat-lining. Labour was haemorrhaging support with its ambivalent stance on the EU. The Tories were tanking so badly their entire strategy appeared to be to pretend the elections weren't even happening. They didn't even bother to have a proper campaign launch.

Time for Gavin Williamson to 'go away and shut up' after leak fiasco

2 MAY 2019

It had been a particularly busy Wednesday evening for Gavin Williamson. In addition to his usual leaking activities, he had had to go through his entire contacts book explaining to everyone how he was innocent of leaking.

Somehow that hadn't seemed quite enough, though, so he had then phoned everyone once more to insist he was also very angry to have been sacked and that he would swear his innocence on his children's lives. To round things off, he'd given an in-depth interview to the *Telegraph* in which he had said he hadn't leaked to the *Telegraph*. Politics at its most meta.

After such an eventful night, the former defence secretary was understandably a little tired. But it was still a shame that he couldn't be bothered to drag himself to the Commons to protest his innocence to his fellow MPs. What better way to convince the world he had been stitched up by the prime minister than with an impassioned, forensic speech from the backbenches. A place where the quality of mercy is often under some strain. Then again, why change the habit of a lifetime? Why tell the truth in public when you can leak it in private?

With Gavin nowhere to be seen, it was left to the de facto deputy prime minister, David Lidington, to explain away the government's latest embarrassment in answer to an urgent question from Labour's Tom Watson. Lidington often gets lumbered with the jobs no one else wants to do and he looked miserable from the start.

This wasn't the Thursday morning he had had in mind. He barely looked up from his notes as he read extracts from the NSC Wikipedia page. 'The NSC was formed 10 years ago,' he mumbled, 'and it's generally accepted that its meetings are kept secret.' With that, he sat down. He'd got through his entire opening statement without mentioning Williamson or the leak once.

Watson wasn't nearly so coy. Either Gavin did it and was banged to rights or he didn't and had been thrown under a bus by Theresa May. Parliament and Gav deserved to know the truth as there had been a serious breach of the Official Secrets Act. So there needed to be a proper criminal investigation. 'Oh no, no, no,' replied a horrified Lidington. That could never happen as the police couldn't do anything unless the government requested it and the government really didn't want to waste the police's time as the secrets hadn't been terribly secret anyway.

Next up was Michael Fallon. Otherwise known as one of the other disgraced former defence secretaries, along with Liam Fox. He was outraged. It was fair enough to be sacked for a bit of #MeToo sex-pestery or treating your chums to holidays at taxpayers' expense: but leaking meetings from the NSC was just a step too far. Williamson had let down the elite club of disgraced former defence secretaries.

It was all downhill from there. Lidington did his best, by first suggesting that there were so many better stories that could have been leaked from the NSC so the government should really be congratulated for its confidentiality and then trying to insist that the cabinet had never been more united. As in united in their hatred and mistrust for one another.

But in the end he just gave up. He didn't really care if Gavin was guilty or not. And neither did the prime minister. It was enough that she had lost confidence in him. Having given him an 18-month probationary period as defence secretary, she had come to the conclusion she didn't much trust him. Or like him. Not only would he never stop going on about how he had been awarded the CBE for twice becoming 'Fireplace Salesman of the Year', he had also accidentally pushed the UK to the brink of war with China. Enough was enough. He was a pain in the arse and it was time for Gav to go away and shut up.

But every cloud and all that. Gavin's loss was Chris Grayling's gain. On another day, the latest no-deal Brexit ferry fiasco would have made front-page news. As it was, there were only a handful of MPs to hear the transport secretary's response to the urgent question. Failing Grayling was as hapless as you might expect. His nervous tic gets more pronounced by the day and his cheek wobbled uncontrollably as he explained how he could easily have wasted even more money. So really everyone should be congratulating him for the dosh he had saved.

Here's the irony. The country can't afford Grayling: he's cost the taxpayer the best part of £3 billion during his time in office. But the Leader In Name Only can't afford to be without him. He never fails to make her look good. He is her therapy support. The dog who gets kicked so she gets off relatively unscathed. He retains her confidence precisely because he is so reliably useless. The faithful fool. Williamson was merely unreliably useless. As Gav would say, sometimes there's no justice.

'NI-GEL!' Brexit party event offers terrifying glimpse of our possible future

13 MAY 2019

'NI-GEL, NI-GEL.'

The Tories have buried their heads in the sand, trying to pretend the European elections aren't really happening next week. Labour has only a slightly firmer grip on reality. Just make it go away. Don't mention the war.

Nigel Farage has never found a political vacuum he wasn't desperate to fill. A voice for any spare, free-floating grievance. The establishment man for the anti-establishment. And at the Featherstone working men's club, he is made to feel right at home. This part of Yorkshire voted nearly 70% to leave the EU and it had been standing-room only long before the Brexit party leader had made his appearance on stage to a saviour's welcome.

'NI-GEL, NI-GEL.'

These days, Farage is being kept on a strict leash by the Brexit party chairman, Richard Tice. Nothing is being left to chance. Even the seemingly unscripted moments are tightly rehearsed. And it was Tice, part millionaire wheeler-dealer, part faux man-of-the-people used car salesman, who opened the rally shortly after 11am with his by now familiar patter of betrayal and humiliation. Politicians, businessmen, the civil service. All of them, enemies of the people. What the country needed was people with the confidence and belief to Make Britain Great Again. A straight lift from the Donald Trump playbook, but no one in the audience cared. They could mainline this stuff all day.

'You couldn't make this stuff up,' yelled the next speaker, John Longworth, the former head of the British Chambers of Commerce and Brexit party candidate for the north-east. Except he did make it up. He lied through his teeth. He told the crowd Brexit had won an overwhelming majority at the referendum, rather than a 52%–48% majority. He told them Westminster was denying them their birthright, forgetting to mention the reason the UK had not already left the EU was because of Brexiters voting down a deal for which they would have given their back teeth three years ago. He told them a no-deal, World Trade Organization Brexit would turn Yorkshire into the land of milk and honey.

Others came and went promising much the same. The local MPs Yvette Cooper and Jon Trickett were booed and openly denounced as traitors. The person to my left to whom I had been chatting before the event advised me not to mention I worked for the *Guardian*. As if I needed telling. This was the blitz spirit being whipped up into a lynch mob. There was a time when a Farage event always came with an element of humour. As if neither he nor his audiences were expected to take him entirely seriously.

This is now something else. Ice-cold calculation tapping into a crowd worn down by austerity and waiting on deliverance. No retreat, baby, no surrender.

Next up was Ann Widdecombe. Under any normal circumstances, a celebrity joke, best known for embarrassing herself as a piss-poor panto act on reality TV shows. A former Tory MP who would have been eaten alive in this Labour stronghold. Instead, she too was greeted with unquestioning adoration. Brexit means Brexit. Democracy betrayed by the rich and the powerful. A lifetime of servitude under the EU. LIES. More lies. She even managed to cram in an impression of Theresa May. That's how bad it's got for the prime minister. To be taken apart by a national joke.

'NI-GEL, NI-GEL.'

Farage acknowledged the applause, his plastic perma-smile stretching into a fixed grin. These weren't really his people, but he needed to make them believe they were. He needn't have worried. The crowd of overwhelmingly white over-50s men and women weren't there to make any demands on him. They just wanted him to sprinkle a bit of stardust their way. Nigel relaxed a little. Though not too much. This was the new, reinvented Farage, not the slightly pissed joker of years gone by. Stay on message. Give them what they want. Then give them more of what they want.

What you get now is Farage from the head, not the heart. A professional politician, masquerading as the outsider and playing the percentages. A man who has spotted an opening and is kicking it ever wider. This wasn't his finest speech, but it didn't need to be. No one was going to ask him any tricky questions about the racism of previous campaigns, his doubts about climate change or how he'd previously advocated a Norwegian-style Brexit. No, he wasn't going to explain exactly how his no-deal Brexit was going to produce untold riches for everyone. Manifestos were only lies anyway. So all he was asking was that they believed and it would come true. And they did believe, because they were that desperate.

'NI-GEL, NI-GEL.'

Here was an all too possible version of the future. One where nuance and complexity have given way to sound-bites and populism. Where lip service is paid to healing divisions, providing it's everyone else who is making the compromises. It was one of the most genuinely disturbing political events I've ever attended. And Westminster ought to be shit-scared.

Change UK is dying before it even learned to walk

16 MAY 2019

A recent opinion poll put Change UK on 2%. What wasn't so clear was whether that figure had been rounded up or down. Just five minutes before its major EU election rally in the Remain heartlands of Bath was about to start, there were still plenty of seats available in the cricket pavilion where it was being held. And there were only 32 chairs to start with. A few late stragglers helped fill the room, but the media still well outnumbered supporters.

Change UK is dying before it even learned to walk. Its MPs know it. Its candidates know it. The public knows it. Change UK never really wanted to change anything. What it wanted most of all was for things to stay the same. For the UK to remain in the EU and for the extremes of both the Tory and Labour parties to shut up and go away.

Now all it wants to change is its name. Change its clothes, its hair, its face. It wants to start again from scratch, to channel the goodwill it generated when its 11 MPs first left their parties and reposition itself as something more positive by forming a tactical alliance with the Lib Dems and Greens. Instead, it now just looks lost. Cut adrift by its own knives. Even its logo of four black lines looks like a subconscious attempt to write itself out of history.

The sound of pan pipes filled the room and a promo film started playing. On a side wall where almost no one could see it. A few seconds in, a circle of death appeared on the wall as the film buffered. Sometimes the metaphors write themselves. It was excruciating. Like intruding on a private grief. The embarrassment only being broken when Sarah Wollaston made a brief introduction and thanked everyone for coming. She might as well have gone round the room and done it in person to everyone. 'We're a very new party,' she said, trying to explain why almost no one was there. Try telling that to Nigel Farage's Brexit party.

Next up was Change UK's top candidate in the south-west, Rachel Johnson. She wisely chose to keep things lightish – God knows everyone needed a bit of cheering up – and started with a dig at Boris. 'At least we've got a bus you can trust,' she began, before segueing into an anecdote about having two Agas. Like her brother, she understands her audience.

But even she couldn't keep it up as the realities became unavoidable and she ended in gallows humour. Change UK were about as dysfunctional as her own family and the polls were so bad it was clear her political career was going to start in failure and that on Sunday week she was going to have, in her own words, her 'arse handed to her on a plate by Ann Widdecombe'. To think, Johnson abandoned the Lib Dems on the grounds that they were absolutely useless. Change UK redefines the very meaning of hope-less. She'll have to work hard to find a better lost cause.

No one can accuse Joan Ryan of indulging in person-ality politics. The former Labour MP is a charisma-free zone, a woman with the air of an over-anxious junior HR manager. The more she tries to encourage you, the worse you feel. She'd make a good living giving eulogies for people she's never met at funeral services where no one has bothered to turn up. It was time someone stuck up for the EU, she said. She was right. Though I suspect everyone in Brussels rather wishes it wasn't her.

'Look at your hands,' she concluded. Everyone briefly woke up, not quite sure they had heard her right. 'Look at your hands,' she again demanded. Everyone rather awkwardly put their hands out in front of them and looked at them. Ryan was thrilled.

'There's the answer,' she beamed. 'The answer is in your hands.' Thank you and goodnight, grasshopper.

Throughout all this, Chuka Umunna had given the appearance of a man trying to pretend he wasn't really there. He had looked disengaged – bored even – staring into the middle distance, as if lost in a private nightmare. Had he really abandoned his political career for this? Sure, he was being hounded out of his Streatham constituency by Momentum activists, but he'd wanted to crash and burn in a blaze of glory. Instead he was just drifting, unnoticed and unmissed, into oblivion. He did gather himself to make something approximating a passionate speech but his stardust wasn't even really working on himself. Chuka, the patron saint of lost causes.

There were no questions at the end. Largely because the only ones worth asking were existential. Why were any of us here at this Change UK event? And not even Change UK had the answers. They are as bewildered by their absence of purpose as the rest of us. But at least they were there. Which is more than could be said of the Tories or Labour, who have more or less abandoned the country. And with the Remain parties most interested in squabbling among themselves, the Brexit party is getting a free pass. Farage must be pissing himself.

* * *

As a last throw of the dice, Theresa May headed off to a central London venue to make one last appeal to her party and the country. She had resigned herself to not getting her own withdrawal agreement through parliament so she was now pitching a deal – any deal – that she thought might stand a chance. Even if parts of the deal appeared to directly contradict one another. She just wanted to win one vote – it didn't matter what on – before she was forced out as prime minister.

Theresa May proves herself the woman who has nothing for everyone

21 MAY 2019

It came billed as the prime minister's 'big and bold' offer. What we got was more of a hostage video. Theresa May's previous major Brexit speeches had taken place in Lancaster House and a Florentine palazzo. Now she was squeezed into the atrium of PWC's offices in Charing Cross, in front of just a handful of pre-selected journalists. Behind the lectern was a map of the world with the words 'Seeking common ground in parliament' written in tiny letters across eastern Turkey, Armenia and Azerbaijan. Presumably because there's a better chance of that there than in the UK.

Shortly after 4pm, May made her way hesitantly in front of the cameras, frequently raising her head towards some bemused accountants on the upper floors – the closest she was going to going to get to a friendly face all afternoon. If only the Four Pot Plants had been able to come along to keep her company. But even they had given up on her. Not that she could blame them. She had all but given up on herself. She was the Leader In Name Only.

'It's a great time to be alive,' she had begun unconvincingly, abject misery written into every line of her face. Brexit is taking its toll on her as well as the country. Only her stubbornness, her refusal to accept the inevitable, was keeping her upright. What she really craved was oblivion. Instead she had to endure humiliation heaped on humiliation. Almost all of it entirely self-inflicted.

What she had to say was too little, too late. A mere repetition of concessions and muddled promises already made. Had she done this six months ago, there might have been a chance of taking the Conservatives – and some Labour MPs – with her. Now she was just screwed. Unloved, unwanted. Too many of her rivals had invested too much time and too much money in their own leadership campaigns to back her now. Her departure was already priced into everyone's timetable. She could have promised almost anything and MPs would have found any number of excuses to reject her withdrawal agreement bill. Wrong font.

Yet still LINO doggedly plodded on. Devoid of charisma, devoid of ideas. Every word dying on her lips. Not so much a prime minister as a supplicant begging for a stay of execution. 'Just let me win one vote,' she begged. That's all she wanted. One victory. By all means trash her WAB (Withdrawal Agreement Bill) at its third reading, just so long as she was given a free pass at the second one. Then she could die happy.

Here was the deal. She'd failed to persuade parliament to accept the deal she had wanted on three occasions, so now she was going to let them vote on a whole load of things she didn't want. Her basic offer was that anything that various groups of MPs had asked for were now all in the mix. Even if some of them were pure fantasy or contradicted one another.

It was all a bit embarrassing. Excruciating even. The backstop would still be in place but it definitely would never be implemented because the brilliant alternative arrangements of the Malthouse compromise – a plan not even its author believed in any more – would come to the rescue. And as for the customs union, she was prepared to give it a bit of a go providing no one called it a customs union and that parliament had a right to opt out of it at the next general election. Which could come sooner than later.

As so often happens, LINO displayed the uncanny knack of simultaneously losing the support of MPs from every side of the argument. The woman who had nothing for everyone. She had never found a crowd that she couldn't alienate. Within days she will have been cast aside by her own cabinet and then she will be entirely adrift. Alone, becalmed, barely afloat. She wasn't even really clear about where she stood on a second referendum. Other than there could be a vote after a vote after another vote. Not enough to please Remainers and far too much for Leavers to accept.

'This is deliverable,' May concluded, even though her new deal was clearly dead on arrival. She looked upwards once more for moral support. But these days, she can't even keep a captive audience. Nearly all the accountants had already wandered off, having long since lost the will to live. There was far more fun to be had from winding up companies bankrupted by a no-deal Brexit than listening to a prime minister's last stand.

After a few desultory, non-committal answers to journalists' questions, LINO sloped back to Downing Street. Yet again she had achieved the seemingly impossible of losing more and more support the longer she spoke. Her deal couldn't even survive contact with her own voice let alone reality. The net was closing in. Time to call in the removal company.

Maybot plods on, each day a greater torment than the last

22 MAY 2019

Many believe that hearing is the last sense to be lost. If true, Theresa May must have been a goner for some time now. She hasn't heard a word anyone has said to her for months. Her cabinet ministers have all but given up trying to explain to her why her Brexit deal won't pass through parliament and have instead taken to communicating with her through a series of placards. All of which say: what part of 'it's time for you to resign' don't you get?

Not that this is proving any more effective, as the prime minister's sight is equally as poor as her hearing. See no evil, hear no evil, speak no evil. The Maybot's vital signs reduced to a random series of ones and noughts, intent only on the basics of minute-by-minute survival. All grasp on reality lost. The living dead.

May frequently makes a point of saying how much she loves her job. One can only wonder at how bad a job would need to be for her to hate it. Her pain threshold must be off the scale. Each day a greater torment than the last. Ridicule from enemies, silence from friends. Anyone with even a smidgeon of self-worth would have quit long ago. But still she plods on, one foot in front of the other, absorbing greater and greater damage. The point where resilience tips into stubborn stupidity long since passed.

There was a time when a prime ministerial statement on Brexit would have guaranteed a full house in the Commons. A moment of national importance. Now it is greeted with widespread indifference. Not only has everyone heard it all before, they also know her withdrawal agreement bill is dead on arrival. The only passing interest is whether it's her or the bill that ends up in the knacker's yard first.

So there were plenty of empty seats – not to mention some attention-seeking flouncing out from Mark Francois – on both sides of the chamber straight after prime minister's questions as May prepared to reprise the speech she had tried out on a handful of sceptical hacks and bored accountants the previous day.

Not least on the government front bench, where Andrea Leadsom, Michael Gove, Penny Mordaunt and Liam Fox had skilfully absented themselves to mastermind *The Maybot: Our Part in her Downfall*. The few cabinet ministers who were present looked like prisoners lined up for a show trial who had guessed the verdict already. All they cared about was trying not to incriminate themselves too much by leaving their fingerprints on the relevant documents.

'This is a deal that MPs can stand behind,' May began. If only in opposition. 'It is time to take decisions, not duck them.' This from a prime minister who had mainlined procrastination for the last three years. She carried on with a selection of not so much her Brexit greatest hits as an album of rubbish B-sides that no one had ever liked. She was heard in near silence. Normally, prime ministers are treated with a veneer of faux respect and sympathy when their days are numbered, but May has forfeited even that doubtful honour. Unloved, unwanted and soon to be unmissed.

The ennui got to Jeremy Corbyn. You might have expected the Labour leader to rise to the occasion and take advantage of the Tory divisions, but he could do no more than go through the motions. He merely phoned in his reply. What she was offering was just more of the same and he couldn't be bothered to engage with it as she was bound to be gone in the next few days or so anyway. And when the Tories did have a new leader he'd make a point of not engaging with him or her either. So much for the UK making the most of its article 50 extension.

What followed were some underpowered speeches from Tory backbenchers, nearly all of which were variations on 'this is crap, you're crap, we're a bit crap' and enlightened no one. A demonstration of existential futility. Politics at its most meta, where everyone has lost the will to say precisely what they mean, so they just fill the time with burbling. No damage was done because there was no more damage that could be done.

The session was predicted to last two and a half hours, but was all wrapped up inside 90 minutes as there was no one still conscious in the chamber. May looked vaguely disappointed. If it had gone on longer, she could have put off all the ministers who were pestering her for a meeting to demand her resignation. Well, sod them all. Sajid, Hunt and Govey could fuck right off. Andrea could walk if she thought she was hard enough. God knows, she'd threatened it often enough in the past. And the 1922 Committee could do one too.

She was going back to barricade herself in Downing Street and hide under the duvet. No one was going to take her alive. Not tonight at any rate. She could be a hero. Just for one more day.

* * *

The European elections were held on Thursday 23 May and even though the votes weren't counted until after 10pm on Sunday to give other countries time to go to the polls, everyone knew the results would be disastrous for the Conservatives. As it turned out they would be even worse than everyone had feared. The Brexit party, led by Nigel Farage, took 30% of the vote and 29 seats, despite having only been in existence for six weeks. The Lib Dems came second with 16 seats, up 15 on their 2014 showing, due to its pro-EU stance. Labour came third, losing 10 of the 20 seats it had previously held, mainly as a result of its muddled position over Brexit, dissatisfaction with the party's handling of antisemitism and loss of faith in

Jeremy Corbyn. The Greens were up three to seven, but the Tories were hammered almost out of sight, winning just four seats, compared to 19 five years previously. Worse even than the pessimists in the Conservative party had feared.

What the European elections principally confirmed was that the country was even more split than ever. The 2016 referendum that had been intended to heal divisions within the Tory party had merely opened them up into a festering sore in the UK at large. The Brexit party and the Conservatives that had been actively campaigning for a hard – or hardish – Brexit scooped up just over 39% of the public vote. The Lib Dems, Labour, the Greens and the Scottish National Party, that had campaigned either to stay in the EU, hold a second referendum or a soft customs union Brexit won just over 48% of the vote. The UK had become a binary nation, split between leaving and remaining in the EU. But what the elections also proved was that Theresa May's time was finally, finally up. No prime minister could hope to remain in office after what her party had suffered – such a humiliating defeat at the hands of the public.

As she says goodbye, Maybot finally shows her humanity

24 MAY 2019

Practice makes perfect. After four previous attempts that had allowed her rather more wriggle room than the Conservative party had been expecting, Theresa May finally delivered her fifth and definitive resignation speech. Arguably it was the best speech she had ever given as prime minister, one that ended with her choking on her words as she tried to contain her tears. Unlike David Cameron, who called time on his career with a jaunty hum – 'Di-dum, di-dee, I didn't do it, it wasn't me, di-dum, di-dee' – May really had given a toss all along. It's just a pity it took her so long to show it.

Shortly after 10am, May walked out into the Downing Street sunshine to inflict the coup de grâce on her time in office. She quickly got to the point. She would be resigning as of 7 June – no one was going to deprive her of a last photo opportunity with Donald Trump – and would step down as prime minister once the Tories had selected a new leader. No ifs, no buts. No more trying to hide inside the fridge at No 10, hoping that her party wouldn't notice she hadn't retreated to Maidenhead as promised. No more blanking out her colleagues in pursuit of the undeliverable deal. This was the end. Beautiful friend, the end.

241

Then came the sting. A hint of defiance. Yes, she might have been one of the worst British prime ministers of the past 200 years, but worse was round the corner. In six months the whole country might beg her to come back. The next prime minister would still have to face the challenge of how to deliver Brexit without bankrupting the UK – and that person could be Boris Johnson, Michael Gove or Andrea Leadsom: three MPs the Tory party rejected three years ago as totally unsuitable to lead the country.

Just imagine Boris as prime minister. A diagnosed narcissist whose entire political career had been constructed through the prism of personal opportunism. A man who as mayor of London had wasted millions of pounds on pointless vanity projects. Who as foreign secretary had insulted the Germans, had contributed to a British national being banged up in Iran and couldn't even take responsibility for a Chequers deal he had signed off. Who had written racist columns in the *Telegraph* and never even aspired to being a man of principle. The populist's populist. Both the thinking man's idiot and the idiot's thinking man. That was the UK's future. Good luck with that. She would be well out of it.

Old habits die hard, though. Either that, or she couldn't resist making time to be her own Maybot tribute act. The defining hallmark of May's time in office has been her binary view of the world. She has always been right and anyone who has tried to contradict her has been shouted down in a meaningless series of monotone ones and noughts. Brexit means Brexit. Strong and Stable. Nothing has changed. A drone in more ways than one. A woman who could make inanimate objects dissolve into tears of frustration.

'Compromise isn't a dirty word,' she observed. Self-knowledge has never been her strongest suit. This from a woman to whom the very idea of compromise is anathema. It had been her insistence on her Brexit red lines that had shaped the whole nature of the withdrawal agreement. It had been her playing to the gallery of the hardline Eurosceptics and her refusal to seek consensus with Remainers that sent her spiralling out of control. Even when she had reluctantly engaged in cross-party talks, her idea of compromise had been to state her position and to expect Labour to fall in line.

Her final plea to be remembered for something other than failing to deliver Brexit fell flat. The best legacy she can realistically expect is to be quickly forgotten, though the country is unlikely to be that forgiving. Her image as the country's therapist and saviour had never been wholly convincing, ever since she had commissioned the 'go home' vans as home secretary.

She tried to run through some of her government's achievements. She needn't have bothered. Successes, she'd had a few. But then again, too few to mention. Her subconscious even compelled her to remember Grenfell Tower. Presumably as an act of atonement. On the day after the fire, she had hidden from the survivors.

After little more than seven minutes at the lectern, May croaked out the last couple of sentences. Here it all became too much and her voice caught in her throat. As the words died on her lips, she turned on her heels and rushed for the front door. Fearful she had revealed too much, when her tragedy had been that she had revealed too little.

Was this the real May or was this just fantasy? No one could be quite certain. Not even the Four Pot Plants who thought they had seen it all. If only the Tories had been sensible enough to select them as their leader, all would have been well. Ish. As it was, Brexit had broken May, just as surely as it would break her successor. A three-year term in office that had started from a seemingly impregnable position of strength had ended in masochistic humiliation. But in losing her job, the Maybot had finally displayed her humanity.

Here was Nigel unplugged. His narcissism and self-deceit exposed

27 MAY 2019

The crack team of UK negotiators lined up for a group photo. Nigel Farage, Richard Tice, Claire Fox, Ann Widdecombe, Annunziata Rees-Mogg and the other 24 new Brexit party MEPs sticking it to the man in the er . . .

imposing establishment surroundings of Carlton House Terrace in the heart of Westminster. But hey, even the men and women of the people need a little down time away from the people they now represent. A chance to chill out and celebrate their success.

These were the names who would strike terror into the Brussels elite. 'So Monsieur so-called Barnier, we are fed up with you humiliating our country,' they planned to say in unison. 'What we demand is that we leave the EU on 31 October on World Trade Organization terms. Nothing more, nothing less.'

'Um . . . OK,' Barnier would then reply. 'If that's what you want, then be our guest.'

'But you don't understand. We are here to negotiate a no-deal Brexit. So we want to do some negotiations.'

'I see. But the whole point of a no-deal is that it doesn't require a negotiation.'

'We don't care. We are the crack team of negotiators. So can we negotiate not having a negotiation?'

Repeat until everyone dies a little more inside. The Brexit party may have the excuse of only being seven weeks old, but you might have thought even they would have thought this one through.

The afternoon after the night before. The Tories had mysteriously chosen not to celebrate their support almost reaching double figures. Instead, Theresa May had posted a desultory tweet about the results being a bit disappointing – since Friday she had better things to do with her life rather than defend her failures – while the nine MPs who had declared their intention to replace her were falling out over who was the best unifying candidate.

Labour, too, was at war with itself over whether or not to support a second referendum as Jeremy Corbyn waited for his advisers to tell him what to think. He hadn't got where he was today by showing leadership. Change UK was about to be taken off life support as the consultants had recommended 'do not resuscitate'. The Greens were off meditating somewhere. The Lib Dems had shot themselves in the foot by arranging their own post-election love-in at precisely the same time as the Brexit party had scheduled theirs some three days earlier. So almost no one turned up. Sometimes it's as if the Lib Dems don't actually want to succeed.

What the EU elections had shown was pretty much what we had already known. That the UK was hopelessly divided. Just over a third of the country wanted a no-deal Brexit, just over a third wanted to remain and the rest wanted some kind of deal but not the one that had been offered. By any normal standards this would be considered a mess. But with the rest of the parties largely missing in action, the Brexit party was happy to rewrite the narrative as a huge success for itself. A Triumph of the Will of the People.

The press conference had been due to take place in a side room overlooking St James's Park. The chairs had all been laid out and the stage prepared for the arrival of Farage and the wannabe shopping channel presenter Tice. But it quickly turned into a complete free for all. For the last seven weeks, Farage has been the model of professionalism, kept on a tight leash by his handlers and sticking resolutely to a few soundbites of betrayal and humiliation. The election over, Nigel was back to his old self. Making it up as he went along and playing to any passing camera as the formal press conference was abandoned while reporters formed a scrum round him at the photocall. You can take the man out of UKIP, but you can't take UKIP out of the man.

'Who here actually wants to take up their seats in Brussels?' Farage asked his assembled MEPs. A few looked as if they were about to raise their arms, before remembering that wasn't the expected answer. But it was hard to blame them as no one looked more thrilled to be going back to the European parliament than Nigel. A place in which he has – in a loose sense – served and drawn a £120k-plus salary for the past 20 years.

Here was Nigel unplugged. His essential narcissism and self-deceit exposed. For years Farage has always insisted his goal is to make himself redundant, but without the attention he gets as a professional politician he could never be sure if he really existed. He feeds off the divisions he creates. The longer he spoke, the more obvious the fault lines became. He claims to want the Westminster politicians to deliver a no-deal Brexit, but is horrified at the thought they might actually achieve it. Because then he would be little more than an ageing picture in the attic.

Today was his day, though. And nothing was going to spoil it. The great disruptor had achieved one of his greatest disruptions. Who cared if he didn't have any policies? Those could wait for another day. Sooner or later some of his MEPs are going to work him out. That there is less to him than meets the eye. That they profoundly disagree with him on key issues. Then it will all start to fall apart. But until then, Nigel will always be a moth to the flame of any microphone. And smile. Fake it to make it.

* * *

Before Theresa May finally stood down there was one last official duty for her to perform. The state visit of the US president, Donald Trump. A visit that had been arranged to make the prime minister look more of a world leader: one that would easily cut a new trade deal with the US once the UK had left the EU. Two leaders ready to carve up the world in their own image. Now all it promised was further embarrassment as everyone knew this was really a sideshow and that May was barely even a supplicant.

Within minutes of landing at Stansted, Trump had courted controversy by tweeting disobliging remarks about the London mayor, Sadiq Khan. He then headed off to the US ambassador's residence in London to watch TV before going to Buckingham Palace to meet the Queen. Not surprisingly, Donald seemed to choose to view his trip to the UK as a glorified holiday, having brought almost his entire extended family along with him for the ride.

On the second day of the state visit, Trump and May had a brief bilateral meeting – there wasn't much to say, given the circumstances – before giving a press conference in the atrium of the Foreign Office. The early part of May's speech was on the impermanence of power. How she and Trump were only temporary guardians of the special relationship. An annihilation of the self. There was no real way back from that and her subsequent attempts to define her legacy were as unconvincing as the achievements themselves. A rare moment of self-knowledge. She had said too much. She hadn't said enough.

Once May had finished and offered the president a handshake, Trump took centre stage. But even he could barely raise a pulse. His mind was elsewhere – reliving the Disney fairytale of meeting the Queen and thinking ahead to more important engagements later that afternoon. Who wouldn't want the wellness spa experience of Piers Morgan crawling up their ass? Sycophantic colonic irrigation. He barely made it through his script, time and again stumbling over words. English is the president's second language. Bollocks being the first.

There was time for some trademark bluster. He and May were probably the biggest business leaders in the entire world. Make that the universe. The US–UK relationship was the greatest alliance ever seen. But even then, his words came with a certain fatigue. As if he was merely going through the motions of being polite, unsure of why the man who made a point of never getting involved with stone-cold losers had found himself on a platform with one.

Things perked up a little when a few questions were invited from the media and The Donald went semi-feral. Sure, he still hated Sadiq Khan – the man should be nicer to him – and he also had no time for Jeremy Corbyn. The Labour leader had requested a meeting – something Corbyn had forgotten to mention when he had turned down the state banquet and had given one of his trademark shouty speeches at a protest rally – but Trump had turned him down. He didn't know him and he didn't like him. So there.

But even this felt underpowered. As if Donald Trump was cosplaying Donald Trump. Of course there were lies. These always priced into every appearance of the US president. He insisted there had been thousands of people cheering for him. There were 100 at most. He was adamant there had been no protesters when there were tens of thousands. #FAKENEWS.

He repeated his claim that he had predicted Brexit when the reality was the result had already been declared when he spoke to the media. There was a time when some would have laughed and others got angry, but now no one cared. Certainly not enough to challenge

him. There was nothing at stake. The press conference of
no more significance than a pre-season football friendly.
Trump's post-truth, alternative facts were no worse than
any other reality.

Throughout all this, May largely kept silent. As if
actively airbrushing herself out of history. Which to all
intents and purposes was what the Conservative party
was already doing as the leadership campaign to replace
her was just about to kick off.

Rory Stewart seems to have forgotten it's the Tories he wants to lead

6 JUNE 2019

It's not immediately obvious that Rory Stewart has got
the hang of this Tory leadership thingy. For the past two
weeks, he has bunked off from the Department for International Development to go walkabout on bridges, in
gardens and in town centres to talk to anyone he can find.
And if no one's around, then he's been as happy to spend
the time using his telescopic arms to film himself talking
just to himself. Sometimes he even agrees with himself.

As a spectacle, it's had a certain charm. Most of the
other leadership contenders wouldn't be seen dead talking
to real people and have devoted their energies to making
campaign videos that veer from the weirdly amateur to

the outright psychopathic. With every new appearance, Dominic Raab increasingly resembles a man who views Hannibal Lecter movies as self-help documentaries. The anger is so barely repressed you expect his hand to explode through the screen and slit your throat. All done with the perfect rictus smile. It's what you would have wanted.

The problem for Stewart is that he has spent most of his time either speaking to the wrong people or saying the wrong things. Because the only people he has managed to win over are the people who would never dream of voting Conservative anyway. He is the candidate everyone who isn't a Tory wants to win the Tory leadership. Appearing compassionate and reasonable – a genial David Attenborough exploring the UK's natural habitats – is not the way to win over the hearts and minds of the Tory grassroots.

A more fundamental error has been that he has failed to understand the rules of the leadership race. The people he most needs to impress aren't the electorate or even the 120k Tory members. They are the 312 other Tory MPs whose support he will need to survive to the final ballot. So far he has just five. Victoria Prentis, Nicholas Soames, Ken Clarke, David Gauke and Antoinette Sandbach. Barely enough to fill a cupboard and too few to make it even to the first round.

On Thursday morning, it appeared Stewart had realised this mistake as, just before he started his day job duties of departmental questions, he had tweeted: 'Now in the House of Commons chamber. Come challenge and ask questions.'

Surely this was his moment to make a pitch to undecided Tory MPs? Only it wasn't. Because he appeared to believe that the MPs he most needed to win over were those on the opposition benches.

Lib Dem Jo Swinson kicked things off by asking about the relationship between international development and the climate emergency. Stewart looked her straight in the eyes. No one was more aware of the need to do more than he was. So much so that it was his intention to double the amount being spent on the climate and the environment. Swinson looked somewhat nonplussed. She had been under the impression Stewart was trying to be Tory leader, but now it looked as if he had switched sides and was staking a claim to the job she was after. The leadership of the Lib Dems.

She hissed a quick 'hands off, pal' before following up with a question on subsidies on fossil fuels. Again, Stewart couldn't have been more accommodating. The government had been hopelessly complacent in this area and Swinson was quite right to point out the contradictions. He was doing everything he could to put things right, but she had to understand that he was limited by the constraints of his ministerial role. He sat down to several loud cheers from the opposition benches.

Having successfully alienated everyone on the Tory benches who would happily destroy the planet for the prospect of a few more years in power, Stewart went fully kamikaze. When the Tory Brexiter Tom Pursglove asked him to set out why the customs union was the wrong policy choice, Stewart told him to get lost. What was most important was that the UK should have zero tariffs and zero quotas access to the EU market.

And another thing . . . while he was about it, he wanted to repeat his conviction that any no-deal Brexit would be suicidal for the UK economy. Thereby wrecking not just his leadership aspirations, but any hopes he might have had of ever serving in the next prime minister's cabinet. That kind of talk will cost lives under a new regime.

Yet by the end of the session, Stewart was all smiles. There was a certain freedom in having been true to himself. Hell, maybe he was a Lib Dem after all. He'd been through worse. Besides, being Rory looked a lot more fun than being Boris, Michael, Jeremy or Psycho Dom. At least he didn't have any lies to remember and could sleep easy at night. Sweet dreams were made of this.

Tory hopefuls prove you don't need to be on drugs to be off your head

10 JUNE 2019

It used to be said that all political careers end in failure. But in the Conservative leadership contest everyone appears to be cutting to the chase by ensuring they start that way as well.

Over the weekend, while almost every contender was busy distancing themselves from their past and insisting it had been a terrible mistake for someone to have discovered they had snorted coke and smoked dope, the one thing on everyone else's mind was the realisation that some Tories clearly don't need to be on drugs to be off their heads. Rather it was the country's tragedy that some of them might not have taken enough. There are frequently more signs of intelligent life to be found in an unconscious MP than a conscious one.

With Theresa May finally out the picture, Matt Hancock was first out the blocks, launching his leadership campaign on the sixth floor of the Royal Festival Hall in London. He bounced on to the stage in a school suit he had grown out of several years previously and proceeded to give his impression of a Silicon Valley social media manager who had spent too much time micro-dosing on psilocybin.

'You are the future,' Tigger said to a room full of reporters. I sincerely hope not or we're even more screwed than I feared. As he spoke his eyes opened wider, pupils dilated, as if imploring everyone to fall into them. The New Age bollocks continued to flow off his tongue. He wanted to provide an emotionally charged platform for something. He had the resilience because you could only do the job if you knew your heart. Om. Obviously he didn't have a coherent Brexit plan because no one does.

He fell to the ground utterly spent. He had given it his all, 110%. By which time his attempts at motivational speaking had sucked the energy out of the entire room. All anyone really wanted to know was whether he had any skeletons in the closet. Tigger looked bewildered. He had none. If only he had said he had done a couple of bank jobs in his teens, he might have been in with a shout of making it past the first round.

An hour later, on the floor below, Maria Miller was introducing the launch of Dominic Raab's campaign. 'He is a man who respects the EU and is respected by the EU,' she said, causing everyone to wonder if she had turned up to the right event. Dom appeared moments later. He'd clearly made an effort, having foregone his regular steroid injections as the crazed psycho stare isn't an altogether winning look, and had come out determined to smile dementedly. Just don't ask him where the bodies are buried.

Now was not the time for foghorn diplomacy, he said. But the EU didn't like it up them and he was the man who would go to Brussels to give everyone a good kicking and salvage the country's pride. He was the conviction Brexiteer you could rely on. To get into a fight. 'We need a buccaneering approach to free trade,' he said. The first candidate to suggest signing a deal with Somali pirates. The price of the pound plummeted against the doubloon. He was last heard talking to himself about World Trade Organization terms and proroguing parliament.

Jeremy Hunt's belief that he was born on the wrong side of the tracks and had to fight his way to the top may be as delusional as many of his policies, but even so he somehow manages to sound like one of the few serious grownups in the room. It's an underrated skill in a politician. Not so long ago, Hunt looked destined to be remembered as the health secretary who knew bugger all about the NHS, but now he has somehow reinvented himself as the person who brought peace to Yemen – something that will comes as news to Yemenis – and as a man with a plan. Even if the plan is to cross his fingers and hope for the best. Not being Boris Johnson can do wonders for a politician's credibility.

As can not being Esther McVey, whose campaign launch consisted of a long rant about how much she hated May, how Lorraine Kelly was jealous of her relationship with Eamonn Holmes and how the failure to deliver Brexit was all the fault of Remainers. All from behind a portrait of Margaret Thatcher.

Her cunning plan to ensure a no-deal Brexit was to not let parliament vote on anything. When she became prime minister the Commons would become a place where people just came for a bit of a natter. Democracy was far too precious to be wasted on democratic institutions. The mainlined vitriol was only halted by a protester declaring McVey was not a true believer in Brexit. There's no pleasing some people.

Alas, poor Michael, we knew him well. Before the hypocrisy surrounding his drug confessions were exposed, Gove had been considered a contender. The Tory capable of going head to head with the newly reclusive

Boris. And everything about his launch event reeked of ambition. No side rooms for him, rather a 28th-floor party venue with a rock'n'roll introductory soundtrack. Queen. Fleetwood Mac. All that was missing were naked dwarves with bowls of coke on their heads.

But when Gove took the stage he looked diminished. A man who knew the game was up. He gave it his best shot, delivering his speech fluently without notes, but his heart wasn't totally in it. The Tory with the pneumatic face had a slow puncture and was vanishing before our eyes.

It was painful to watch. Mikey went through the familiar spiel. His mission was to unlock people's potential. Westminster is littered with the corpses of politicians who have made that promise. If it was that easy, someone might have managed it by now. He didn't quite know what his Brexit plan was, but he was sure something might turn up. If not by 31 October then shortly afterwards. It had sounded so much more convincing when he had rehearsed it in front of the mirror. If only that had been the only thing he had done in front of a mirror.

Mikey did liven up a little with a few well-aimed swipes at his nemesis towards the end. Boris should not pull out this time. Snarf, snarf. Johnson was a man whom the country simply could not trust. Unfortunately, the country had come to the same conclusion about him. It was second time unlucky for Gove. Three years ago he had knifed Boris in the back. Now he had done the same thing to himself. Some might call it karma.

More merry pranksters take the Tories' Electric Fool-Aid Acid Test

11 JUNE 2019

Day two in the Big Brother house. The chimps are still completely out of control and have started throwing food and worse at one another. Would Andrea please come to the diary room?

No one could accuse Andrea Leadsom of not learning from her mistakes. When she first ran for the Tory leadership, she made a point of inviting everyone to witness her campaign launch. It featured a 'major speech on the economy' in which she didn't once mention the economy and a march on Westminster comprising just her, Tim Loughton and Theresa Villiers. Once seen, never forgotten. That one joint she smoked at university must have had a devastating long-lasting effect on her.

This time round, though, Leadsom was taking no chances. Her launch took place in a Westminster broom cupboard to which several journalists, myself included, were refused entrance. The venue was full, we were told. All 15 seats were already reserved. Only that wasn't quite true. There were still empty chairs by the time Leadsom appeared on stage to talk. To herself, if no one else.

What wasn't so clear was why she imagined she was any better suited to being prime minister now, having crashed and burned so spectacularly first time around. The only possible conclusion was that she reckoned that in the intervening three years the idiot bar had lowered significantly.

Leadsom looked up nervously. She wanted people to be the very best they could be. Unlike last time when she had wanted them to be the worst they could be. Nothing escapes Andrea.

And she had an absolutely foolproof Brexit plan. She would tell parliament she had a really shit, unworkable plan and that if they did not want to vote for it then she had an equally shit plan for no-deal. But not to worry, as there was no chance of her becoming prime minister.

'Who am I?' she asked. It was a very good question. But if she didn't know, there was precious little chance of anyone in the audience being able to help her out. Assuming they actually gave a toss. The BBC certainly didn't, gleefully curtailing its coverage to go to a story about an escaped hamster. Or something. By the time the Beeb cut back to Leadsom five minutes later, she had all but wrapped up her launch.

There was an awkward silence at the end before a couple of admirers led a round of desultory applause. No #Rally4Leadsom glory days this time round. The ever-loyal Loughton trudged back to Westminster alone, quietly sobbing to himself: 'Who do we want? Andrea Leadsom.' Where had it all gone wrong? Maybe next time. There would be a next time. Wouldn't there?

Half an hour later, in another room in the same building – presumably there had been a buy one, get one free offer – Mark Harper strode purposefully to the front and took off his jacket. As if to say: here is a man who means business. Who would give straight answers to straight questions. The first of which was just who the hell he was. Not even his family always got that one right.

'Aha,' said Harper. The very fact he was completely unknown – other than for having had to resign as immigration minister for employing an illegal immigrant – was what made him just the person to lead the Conservatives and deliver Brexit. He would just wander up to Angela Merkel and say: 'Hi, I want to do a deal,' and she would reply: 'Sure. Danke fuck you aren't Boris or Michael or Jeremy.' And that would be that. A deal would be done sometime in the next six months or so. It was no more incredible than anything anyone else had come up with.

No, he hadn't done any drugs, he added, wistfully. He'd longed to join in with all his colleagues doing lines of coke – Mikey was a total blast when he was off his head – and smoking dope. But he'd just never been invited to the right parties. That was why his campaign slogan was 'Time for a party where everyone is invited'.

It wasn't long before the only question anyone could think to ask was whether a lion would beat a bear in a fight. Harper deliberated for a few moments. 'Lion,' he said. Koala bears everywhere cheered wildly. They'd never had it so good. The state of the Tory party. The state of the country.

Humiliated by its own government, by its own pretenders. Harper sidled off, never to be seen again. It had been a short and sweet campaign. In its way, a collector's item.

Something rather more hallucinatory was on offer later. Tugging on his opium pipe, Rory Stewart had hired a circus tent on London's South Bank. To go out with a bang. Or a bong. And what visions Rory the Ringmaster had on offer to a packed house of 600! Here was a possibility of a united Britain. A Xanadu where people came together to settle their Brexit differences through a citizens' assembly. Where people felt a sense of shame at the state of hospitals, schools and prisons. Where conviction and seriousness walked hand in hand. Where binary politics dissolved into a purple haze of peace and love.

It was by far the best speech any Tory candidate had made. One which offered a real sense of leadership. Only it will never catch on, as the party Rory the Ringmaster wants to lead is not the Conservative party. It's the Lib Dems, or something like them. And in his heart he knows that. Towards the end, when the visions were less intense, reality began to seep in. He admitted that his middle ground was a lost cause in a contest where Boris Johnson was favourite. The Ringmaster was no match for the elephant. Whether in the room or out. He even said he would back a Labour bill to take no-deal and prorogation off the table.

And with that the dream really did die. It was a matter of when, not if, his campaign turned to ash. The Electric Fool-Aid Acid Test would have to carry on without him.

Boris Johnson is every bit as dull and evasive as his minders hoped

12 JUNE 2019

The instructions from his minders had been clear. Keep it dull, keep it vague and get the hell out of the room as fast as possible. They hadn't gone to the trouble of keeping their man away from the media for weeks on end, only for him to blow it on his first outing. The last thing they wanted was for Boris Johnson to be the real Boris Johnson. His serial dishonesty, his total untrustworthiness and sheer incompetence were best kept under wraps, at least until after he became the prime minister. What was required for his campaign launch was a hollowed-out Boris. Someone who could near enough pass himself off as credible.

Geoffrey Cox, a man with a long track record of defending the indefensible, took to the stage of a crowded, overheated room in Westminster to get proceedings under way. This was a time of great crisis for the country, he intoned in his trademark cod-Shakespearean baritone. Cox never tires of hearing his own voice. The next prime minister needed to be a person of the very highest calibre. Someone who could unite the country. Someone of the soundest character. Despite all this, he was still going to back Boris. Because the leadership contest had only ever been about the survival of the Tory party. And Johnson was the only lifeboat in view.

Moments later a crumpled, ashen Johnson appeared to a standing ovation of dozens of Tory MPs. At which point it became clear this wasn't so much a leadership launch as a jobs fair for the not very talented. It's quite something when Liz Truss, Gavin Williamson and Chris Grayling are three of the brightest people in the room. Near the back, large numbers of the European Research Group and a few token Remainers bounced up and down, desperate to be noticed.

'Piffle, poffle, wiffle, waffle,' Johnson mumbled, tugging on a sweaty strand of hair. His minders purred. This was every bit as boring and low key as they had hoped. Most of the audience were dozing off long before their man had finished his first sentence, and even Boris was having trouble keeping his eyes open. Backstage, someone turned the heating up another couple of notches. Just to maintain the torpor.

There was one tricky moment when Johnson talked about the need to have a strict moral purpose. Two words that have never knowingly been applied to him. Not even his own family trusts him to tell the truth. His family especially don't trust him to tell the truth. They know everything is all about Boris. Always has been, always will be. His narcissistic personality disorder makes it impossible for him to view other people as anything more than satellites of his own ego.

Sensing he was veering towards dangerous territory, Johnson switched tack. 'Piffle, poffle, wiffle, waffle,' he mumbled. He was going to get a good Brexit deal because EU trade negotiations were based on the Hegelian dialectic. The more the EU distrusted a prime minister, the more likely it was to offer the UK everything we asked for. But if by any chance he couldn't get a deal by 31 October then he was quite happy to leave with no deal. He wisely kept his fingers firmly crossed.

Johnson couldn't help looking a bit disappointed when he concluded his speech. His one nation appeal had always felt tenuous and no one appeared convinced. He was used to entertaining people and felt deprived without unconditional acclaim. This was more of a business transaction. His need to be prime minister in exchange for MPs' need to keep their jobs. Even he could sense there was something rather grubby about it. Three years previously, he had had a brief window of self-awareness in which he had realised he was totally unfit to lead the country. Now his dysfunction and denial were back up and running. He would destroy himself and he would destroy the country. A massive ego with zero self-esteem.

'I'll take just six questions,' he said. Six too many as far as his handlers were concerned, but far too few for a media and public who felt that every candidate should be subject to proper scrutiny. Not that Johnson had any intention of answering questions. Rather, he retreated to his default setting. Jokey and evasive.

No, he didn't want to talk about his record at the Foreign Office. Probably because his tenure had been an unmitigated disaster. Rather, he wanted to claim other people's achievements during his time as London mayor as his own. And no, he couldn't say if he would resign if the UK was still in the EU on 31 October. Just stop asking difficult Brexity questions. Let Brexit lie. Let him lie. Lying was what he did best.

There were loud boos from Mark Francois and many other MPs when Johnson's character was questioned. Shouting down journalists marked a new low, even for Boris. Vote Johnson, get Trump. Johnson didn't care much either way. Instead he argued that he was only saying what most people thought. And he was nothing if not a man of the people. So he would continue calling women in burqas letterboxes and gay men bum boys. BUM BOYS. BUM BOYS. So there. And when he'd said 'fuck business' he'd meant it as a compliment.

Just as the event threatened to unravel, Johnson remembered his instructions and dashed for the exit. Some journalists shouted that the whole event had been a total disgrace, but for Boris it had done the business. He had got through the day more or less unexamined. Onwards and downwards, further into the cesspit of Tory party politics.

The strongarm tactics pay off for smirking Team Boris

13 JUNE 2019

Shortly after he had tweeted that it felt like his wedding day all over again, Jeremy Hunt walked into Committee Room 14 to cast his vote. Presumably his wife picked her husband in a secret ballot. Moments later, Dominic Raab followed him, the anger vein pumping overtime in his forehead. He was rushing on his steroid run. And he felt just like Jesus's son.

Other MPs had their phones confiscated at the door. There had been rumours that Team Boris, led by Gavin Williamson, had instructed all their supporters to take a picture of their ballot paper with the X in the appropriate box. Trust is currently in short supply in the Tory party, and many MPs appear shell-shocked by the viciousness of the threats being made in private in the Commons tea rooms. More savvy MPs came ready with a burner phone. A WhatsApp photo message could be the difference between a ministerial career and the backbenches.

Theresa May muttered a brusque: 'None of your business' when asked whom she had voted for, while Michael Gove declared he had voted for the best candidate. Which must be the first time a leadership contender has openly admitted he wouldn't be voting for himself.

Boris Johnson, mouth clamped shut with gaffer tape, arrived with a minder whose sole job was to ensure his man said nothing to anyone. Mission accomplished. The less Johnson says in public, the more Tory MPs flock to support him.

Of the contenders themselves, only Esther McVey, Andrea Leadsom and Rory Stewart were ever-presents in the corridor. McVey and Leadsom kept their heads down, as if already resigned to their fate, while Stewart paced nervously. It soon became clear why. His big beast supporter, Ken Clarke, had gone AWOL and didn't have a phone. With just 15 minutes to go till voting closed, Clarke finally appeared. Stewart looked a relieved man.

David Davis had been forced to make a second attempt at voting, the first having ended in failure when he couldn't produce any ID. 'We don't know who you are, David,' one of the tellers had said. He didn't seem that bothered and used the opportunity to audition for his one-man standup show. How had the PM voted? 'I've no idea. And I had a drink with her last night.' Was he campaigning for Raab? Not when he had been having a drink with Theresa. Boom, boom. Don't call us.

Only Raab and Stewart bothered to turn up in person for the result shortly after 1pm. The declaration was made by Cheryl Gillan, as the chairman of the 1922 Committee, Graham Brady, had recused himself to stand in the election, only to fail to secure enough supporters to even make it on the ballot. A man who gives hope to us all. He fails so we don't have to. Westminster's very own Prince Andrew.

Then the spinning started. Team Boris said little and tried not to smirk. The margin of victory had exceeded even their own expectations. Williamson's strongarm tactics had paid dividends. Hard to imagine anyone being terrified by Private Pike, but there's no accounting for the vices and self-interest of Tory MPs.

Sajid Javid's adviser insisted her man had finished 'a very strong fifth' by picking up 23 votes. She didn't look best pleased when several journalists, myself included, started sniggering. 'It's true,' she said crossly. 'At one point he was in sixth place.' It wasn't the strongest of sales pitches.

Silence is golden as Boris's lectern wins Tory televised debate

16 JUNE 2019

Father's Day is always a tricky occasion in the Boris Johnson households, so it was perhaps understandable he chose to send along a lectern to represent him at the Channel 4 Tory leadership debate instead. It proved to be an inspired move, because the lectern answered the questions far more directly and honestly than Johnson ever would. If only the lectern had taken his place at the foreign affairs select committee, there's a good chance

Nazanin Zaghari-Ratcliffe would have been released from her Iranian jail by now.

Curiously, everyone but Jeremy Hunt chose to ignore the fact that the odds-on favourite to become the next prime minister was otherwise engaged. And he only appeared to notice about halfway through with a slightly embarrassed, 'Where's Boris?' It was as if someone had shat themselves and everyone was too polite to mention it. Which, come to think of it, was more or less exactly what had happened. Still, at least it gave the others some more airtime. Not that it did many of them much good.

It's been a good 20 years or so since Michael Gove last did cocaine, but he appeared to be still suffering from the after-effects. Angry, edgy, wired and shouty. Asked to take the first question on how he would win an election against Nigel Farage and Jeremy Corbyn he merely insisted he would win because he was the best, and became increasingly bewildered and tetchy when nobody clapped anything he said. 'I've put everything on the line,' he later added. Under the circumstances, not the best choice of words.

Things began to turn nasty when the questions turned to Brexit as Gove, Hunt, Sajid Javid and Dominic Raab tried to outdo one another with how hard they were. A contest in which there was only ever going to be one winner. Raab had clearly been briefed to try to remember to smile but it wasn't long before the anger vein on his forehead was throbbing as the steroids coursed through his veins. When Rory Stewart called him out for being deranged, it looked as if Raab was seconds away from taking an axe to him. And then taking out the entire audience. The new muscular Conservatism.

'I'm an entrepreneur,' Hunt replied irrelevantly to almost every question. He didn't look much like a businessman. With his Union Jack lapel badge he seemed more like a British Airways senior cabin steward on a long-haul flight. Javid wisely chose not to mention that he'd made a fortune as a banker selling credit default swaps in the run-up to the financial crisis, but still tried to pull macho rank. He was a man who got things done even through he couldn't point to anything he'd actually got done. Needless to say, throughout all this no one was able to explain just how they were going to deliver Brexit. So no one was the wiser about anything.

About an hour in, despite the best efforts of presenter Krishnan Guru-Murthy to jolly things along, the debate began to flag rather. Each candidate sobbed gently at the current state of the education, health and social care system, apparently unaware they had been responsible for their decline over the past nine years. Suddenly, the *Poirot* repeat on ITV 3 seemed an attractive option. Thank God for the adverts, which included a trailer for *Celebrity Crystal Maze*. The comparisons were unmissable. A bunch of chimps would stand more chance of working as a team than the five Tories on show.

Things did perk up with a leftfield question about what each man considered to be his weakness. Gove went first. 'Impatience,' he snarled. Along with modesty. He was such a go-getting, high achiever that people had trouble keeping up with him.

'As an entrepreneur,' sobbed Hunt. People sometimes thought he was a pushover, but actually he was a real hardman. Just ask the bloke in seat 27F who hadn't worn his seat belt. Javid's confession was that he should have bought the family a dog sooner. Really. Raab twitched shiftily. Now probably wasn't the time to mention he had multiple convictions for road rage attacks.

At which point, Stewart stole the show. He was frail. He was ignorant. Other people knew more than him. He sometimes changed his mind. Now it wasn't just Raab who wanted to kill him. All the others did too. Why hadn't they thought of talking human? The audience gave Stewart a loud round of applause. As indeed they had all night. Rory fluttered his eyelids and smiled bashfully. He'd won the debate hands down, but it would count for little. His electorate wasn't either the audience or the viewers. It was the other Tory MPs and members and they had long since made up their mind. The lectern had it.

Ageing boy band's reunion manages to hit all the wrong notes

18 JUNE 2019

He speaks. And yet he still says nothing. Given that he has been held hostage by his minders for the past few months, it was only fair that Boris Johnson was given the chance to answer the first question on the BBC's Tory leadership debate. 'Piffle, paffle, wiffle, waffle,' said the pasty-faced, priapic Mr Blobby. His time in captivity has played havoc with his complexion.

And with his thought processes. Asked to explain if he would leave the EU on 31 October, Johnson managed to both say he would and he wouldn't. Much the same as he has been telling both his Remainer and Leaver supporters. Only the public are less gullible than some Tory MPs. 'Politicians need to act seriously and soberly,' he concluded, trying to remember not to smirk. Thereby in effect ruling himself out as the UK's next prime minister. Only for Jeremy Hunt, Michael Gove and Sajid Javid to do much the same. Rory Stewart sounded a little less deranged, but his Brexit plans don't stand much scrutiny either.

It was all downhill from there. The five men were all sitting on stools, as if they were an ageing boyband performing a one-off reunion gig. Take Twat. Ten minutes in,

Stewart began to undress by taking off his tie and that's when the old artistic differences really kicked.

'Your ideas are really shit,' said one.

'No they're not,' said another.

'It's your ideas that are shit.'

'It's my turn to be on lead vocals.'

'Well stop singing out of tune.'

'You're back on the coke.'

The entire audience, which was already rapidly thinning out as more and more people switched over to repeats of *Chernobyl* for light relief, wished they were back on barbiturates. At one point, the presenter, Emily Maitlis, looked as if she too had had enough and wanted to walk off the set. But her professionalism kicked in as Take Twat continued to talk over one another and squabble among themselves.

'Has that answered your question?' Maitlis asked James from Belfast after Mr Blobby and the Blobbettes had argued over GATT 24, sheep farming and other things about which they clearly knew nothing.

'Not really,' said James, committing hara-kiri. He spoke for an entire nation.

Having given up any hope of getting a straight answer on Brexit, other questions came in on tax cuts, Islamophobia and public services. Bizarrely, one man even thought Hunt had given a satisfactory reply. Ken Doll lookalike Hunt appeared amazed by this. It wasn't his style at all.

'Could you just tell me whether my husband will be OK?' pleaded Carmela from Southampton. 'Your husband is toast,' snapped Gove. 'He can piss off and die. Now stop talking while I'm interrupting.'

It was a relief when it all ended. Not even a near-naked, straight-talking Stewart could chalk this one up as a success. All the country had learned was that it wished they would all shut the fuck up and it didn't want any of them as prime minister. The only winner on the night was Jeremy Corbyn.

The final line-up for Take Twat had been decided at the second round of voting earlier in the day. Yet again Stewart had been the first candidate to show his face and remained in the corridor throughout the two hours. Pacing, pacing, always on the move. Walking is what he does. Was he feeling confident? If he told you, he'd have to kill you. Wet jobs R'Us. 'Ah,' he said. 'There goes Damian Green. Just the sort of person who would vote for Boris unless I look him in the eye.' Too late. Green had already voted for a return to cabinet.

Dominic Raab came and went without saying a word. As did Boris Johnson. 'Can't you even smile?' someone asked. He couldn't. It was more than the job he wanted was worth. He'd almost certainly screw up at some point, but not just yet. Ken Doll forced a grin. Gavin Williamson had promised to loan him some of Boris's votes to make sure he was safe.

The Team Boris camp had banged the table enthusiastically when Matt Hancock turned up. Quite how the health secretary sleeps at night is anyone's guess. He must have been promised one hell of a promotion. Rumours are that he wants to be chancellor. Which could be a problem as Boris has already promised that to several other of his supporters. It looks like a Johnson government is going to involve a lot of family-friendly job sharing.

Then came the result. Hunt and Michael Gove had stalled, Sajid Javid's dog had just scraped over the line. Raab was out and the police were out in force in case he went on a killing spree in Westminster. So much pent-up anger surely had to be released. The only one to have outperformed expectations had been Stewart. The pacing had paid off. The outsider 007 would live to die another day.

Farewell realism's Rory Stewart – elbowed out by chancers and charlatans

19 JUNE 2019

Shortly after six o'clock on Wednesday, Charles Walker, the joint acting chair of the 1922 Committee, confirmed what most people had already suspected. Rory Stewart was out of the leadership contest, his support having haemorrhaged away. The Tories had looked the national interest in the eye and put the party first.

The one candidate who had injected some realism into the race had been sharp-elbowed in favour of a bunch of incompetent charlatans, chancers and jobsworths. Men selling impossible dreams to the intensely gullible. #RoryWalksOn had become #RoryWalksOff. Though his time might come again. Possibly even later this year.

As in the previous rounds, voting had begun at 3pm but this time there was a difference. No Stewart. Normally the Walking 007 is one of the first on the scene, patrolling the corridor, peering deep into the souls of wavering Tory MPs. Daring themselves to put their consciences before their careers. Almost always a pointless exercise, but it keeps him occupied. The place felt empty without him. The chronicle of a death foretold.

First of the candidates to appear was Ken Doll, Jeremy Hunt. Still composed, fixed smile in place. Still wearing his neatly pressed BA senior cabin steward's uniform. How was he feeling? Doors to manual, he replied automatically. His campaign could do with an upgrade.

Sajid Javid came and went surrounded by his own team, like some kind of mafia don. Overnight he'd lost his principles, come out swinging hard for a no-deal Brexit on 31 October to win over Dominic Raab's psychonaut supporters and looked all the more chipper for it.

Once the contest was over, he'd even have the sodding dog put down. He'd never much liked it, but it had been worth some votes. Raab himself looked chastened. But then anyone would if they were out on police bail in connection with the murder of five people, whose bodies had turned up in the Thames the night before.

Next in was Michael Gove, who has also perked up now he appears to be in recovery from his drug hell. The Narcotics Anonymous meetings have clearly been doing him a power of good. He has just about mastered Step One, his powerlessness over his unsuitability to be prime minister, but has a lot of work to do on his character defects. Where to begin with them?

Westminster's very own priapic Mr Blobby, Boris Johnson, yet again said nothing as his courtiers danced around him, parading their undying loyalty as if to some Tudor king.

There's going to be a lot of disappointed MPs when the inevitable coronation takes place in July. Matt 'Gizza Job' Hancock was taking no chances. The former Remainer, now hardline 'Bring it on Michel, if you think you're hard enough' Eurosceptic, proudly displayed the burner phone he'd taken into the voting booth with him. A photo had already been sent to Mr Blobby's campaign manager, Gavin Williamson.

An hour later Walking Rory finally wandered into view. He apologised for his absence. He had been down in the tearooms, begging for support. Did he have enough? 'Who knows?' he shrugged, as he had in the previous rounds. But this time he sounded as if he really meant it.

He was worried about one proxy voter, but thought he might have picked up a couple more supporters from Raab. And yes, he wished he had done better in the debate the night before, but it wasn't easy when you had four mad people telling you you were mad. His Brexit plans may be just as unrealistic as everyone else's, but at least he talked human.

Yet again, Theresa May refused to disclose how she had voted, once more telling a crowd of journalists to mind their own business. She must have been tempted to say she had voted for Mr Blobby. Just about the only thing that could stop Johnson from becoming the next prime minister was a gushing endorsement from the present occupant of No 10.

There again, the emeritus prime minister could just be sadistic enough to want Johnson to experience the full hubris of his ambition, knowing that he was bound to screw up big time sooner rather than later and that the Tories would be ruthless in removing him. She certainly hadn't been in the mood to defend Mr Blobby's reputation at a sparsely attended PMQs.

After struggling to answer some well-directed questions from Jeremy Corbyn about Grenfell Tower – who would have guessed that setting up a public inquiry might not cut it or that private landlords might not be too bothered about dangerous cladding? – May found herself on the receiving end of a tirade from the SNP leader Ian Blackford about Johnson's racism.

Several Tory MPs feigned outrage that a man who had made frequent racist remarks should be labelled a racist, but May merely demurred. Tory MPs had made it clear they wanted a racist fantasist as their next leader. They could reap what they had sown.

Bumbling Boris Johnson takes to the airwaves to lie, lie and lie again

25 JUNE 2019

You can see why Boris Johnson's carers have chosen to mothball him in recent weeks. His decline has been almost total. Johnson never did much care for the past or the future. Every day has always been a tabula rasa, one on which he was free to reinvent himself as he pleased without being bound by any commitments he may have made. Now though, he appears to barely have a present. Unable even to maintain the most basic rules of conversation, his words are just a scattergun of free association.

Nick Ferrari began Johnson's LBC radio interview with a few easy rapid-fire yes-or-no questions as if to establish a benchmark for the lie detector. It proved hard work as Johnson was such a shambles he could barely even confirm his name. Was he a coward? That should have been a no-brainer. That's the one thing on which everyone – even his friends – agree. Johnson merely looked confused. The silence was interpreted as a yes on the polygraph.

Having made some kind of progress, Ferrari moved on to the staged photograph of Johnson and Carrie Symonds in a Sussex garden. Did he know who had taken the picture? 'Um . . . er . . . ,' mumbled Boris. There had been so many photos and so little time. Could he even remember when the photo was taken? A look of panic crossed his face. When you've told so many lies, there's always a danger you might accidentally tell the truth.

Look, said Ferrari, the hair's all wrong in the photo. It's much longer than it is now. So this picture was taken months ago. You've been taking the public for fools. 'Um ... er ... crikey,' Johnson stammered, trying to rediscover the inner clown tribute act which had proved such a winner in the early years of his political career. The thing about his hair ... The thing about him was he was so virile – literally overflowing with spunk at times – that his hair grew incredibly fast and he sometimes had to have it cut two or three times a day.

There was no more coherence from Johnson when listeners were invited to have their say. Especially on Brexit. The man Tory MPs have staked their careers on is literally clueless about Brexit. His ignorance near total. First, he would get the EU to admit the withdrawal agreement was nonsense. Then he'd set up some badger border patrols in Northern Ireland. As for the £39 billion, he'd treat it with some creative ambiguity. Much like his relationships. A need-to-know basis.

But how can we trust you, asked Mike from Littlehampton. You were rubbish as London mayor and rubbish as foreign secretary. 'Um ... er ... wiffle ... waffle ... ,' Johnson bumbled, a bead of sweat appearing on his brow. The thing about trust was that it was over-rated. People had tried voting for politicians they trusted and that hadn't worked out, so now it was time for someone who could be relied on to let you down and not tell the truth. The kind of unreliability you could trust.

Close to the end, as the interview disintegrated into a gestalt therapy session, Johnson broke down. 'People are trying to stop me achieving what I want to achieve,' he sobbed. Finally the mask had dropped and we had the real man. One with the limitless sense of entitlement who believes that normal rules do not apply to him. Being prime minister was only ever a box to tick on his CV. An ego trip of narcissistic self-gratification. It had never occurred to him that being prime minister was about other people's needs. It had only ever been about him.

Johnson was still a complete wreck an hour later when he gave a second interview to TalkRadio's Ross Kempsell. Now he didn't even bother trying to talk in proper sentences. He had regressed so far he was pre-verbal. 'Do or die,' he snapped. Brexit as Biggles book. He would do and the rest of us could die. Yes, he might have been slung out by his wife. Yes, the police might have been called to his girlfriend's flat. Yes, he was basically dossing on the floor, living out of a suitcase with his underpants only held together by the stains. But in his mind he was Mummy's 'King of the World'.

Then came the final implosion. Asked what he liked to do in his spare time, Johnson literally had no idea what to say as even he could see that 'shagging' wasn't an appropriate answer. 'Um . . . er . . . ,' he said. He liked making buses from wooden crates. No, not crates, but cardboard boxes. Then he coloured them in red, wrote £350 million down the side, and painted in happy faces of people all saying how much they loved Boris before breaking into a chorus of 'The Wheels on the Bus Go Round and Round'. Call it occupational therapy for a sex and love addict.

Kempsell understandably looked amazed. Even Johnson looked as if he had surprised himself. It was such a pointless, obvious lie. One there had been no need to tell. But he just couldn't help himself. Lying was what he did. Lying was what he had always done. And it would almost certainly earn him the keys to Downing Street. In the meantime, one of his carers was sent off to make a cardboard bus. Just so they would have something to show the media.

We'd be better off picking someone at random and giving them keys to No 10

9 JULY 2019

There was a brief frisson of excitement when someone said that Jason McCartney was in the spin room for the ITV leadership debate in Manchester. No one knew the former North Melbourne Aussie rules footballer and current list manager at the Greater Western Sydney Giants was in town. Then the excitement died a little. It was a different Jason McCartney. Jason McCartney, the former Tory MP who lost his seat at the 2017 general election and was now delegated to be cheerleader in chief for Team Boris. Point man to explain to a room full of hacks why his man had won the debate. Even if he hadn't. Understandably McCartney looked slightly overawed by the responsibility.

Over on the other side of the room rooting for Team Hunt was another former MP, Rob Wilson. Him and me neither. It hadn't been meant to be like this. The spin room had been billed to be full of ambitious Tory MPs, slavering for top jobs when their man became prime minister. Except it turned out that the Conservative whips hadn't quite trusted their Labour counterparts to pair their absentee MPs and had ordered them all back to Westminster for the crucial vote on the Dominic Grieve amendment to force parliament to report fortnightly throughout October. Even then it hadn't been enough as the government was defeated by a single vote. A sign of things to come.

The debate proper began with both men appearing on stage like two contestants in a dodgy 1980s game show. Boris Johnson stared at the floor. A man-boy dressed in an ill-fitting suit. Don't mess this up, he told himself. All he needed to do was get through the next hour and he would end up as prime minister. 'Pifflepafflewifflewaffle,' he babbled. On reflection, taking a large amount of amphetamines just minutes before going on air hadn't been that good an idea. Jeremy Hunt was in full psycho Colonel Kurtz mode.

Eyes fixed and jaw clenched. A cocktail of steroids and napalm was a heady mix. He was the entrepreneur with a plan. The first health secretary to have run the NHS. Into the ground.

That pretty much turned out to be the highlight of the entire show – apart from the ad break – with Johnson choosing to treat proceedings like a third-rate debate at the Oxford Union. 'I've got a four-point plan,' he shouted. No one had apparently told him he was wearing a microphone. 'Well, I've got a 10-point plan,' Hunt countered. Boris looked rather put out. The fact that neither plan bore any close examination was neither here nor there.

Colonel Kurtz then went on the offensive. Would Boris resign if he failed to deliver Brexit by 31 October? PIFF-FLEPAFFLEWIFFFLEWAFFLE. Was that a yes or no? PIFFLEPAFFLEWIFFLEWAFFLE. We all just needed to believe. In something. Anything. Be optimistic. So long as it included Boris becoming prime minister. When in doubt make a gag. Classic deflection tactics. It was a pitiful object lesson in failing to answer any serious questions. A show of entitled, showman arrogance. In a contest that involved more than 160,000 Tory members, it could have proved fatal. As it was, he could almost say anything. Most of the votes were already in.

'Yes he does,' snarled Kurtz.
'No, he doesn't,' snapped Johnson.
'Does.'

'Doesn't.'

Feeble doesn't begin to do it justice. It would have been more enlightening had both men stripped to their boxers and started arm-wrestling. Giant Haystacks versus Little Daddy. The host Julie Etchingham, who was rapidly emerging as the evening's runaway winner, let out a primal scream of pain. As she tried to stop the two men squabbling, it gradually dawned on her that one of these men was going to wind up as prime minister. The country really was screwed. We'd be better off picking someone from the audience at random and give them the keys to No 10.

Kurtz did try to get more serious, but each time Johnson merely smirked. Fantasy answers to genuine questions was all he could manage. No one was more relieved than Etchingham when the clock ticked round to the last question. What quality did both men admire in the other? Boris was silent. As a paid-up narcissist he'd never given anyone other than himself a moment's thought. 'Um ... um ...' he's alive. Hunt merely mocked Johnson's continued inability to answer questions. He might once have fancied a job in Boris's cabinet, but now not so much. An hour up close and personal was more than enough.

The closing credits rolled and Boris heaved a sigh of relief. Sure he'd been shit – he'd shown his angry, spiteful, bullying side – but not shit enough to make a difference. The Tory members really were that mad.

Just as planned, he'd got away by acting like a guilty 12-year-old caught playing the clown. Over at ITV headquarters, the controller broke down in tears. He had cleared the schedules for this. For this. He should have stuck to *Love Island*.

It will be Boris Johnson. And it will certainly be a disaster

15 JULY 2019

It could just have been overconfidence. More likely it was a white flag. A giving in to the inevitable. For the final head-to-head debate in the Tory leadership race, Team Hunt hadn't sent a single MP out into the spin room to explain why their man was about to win. Not even Liam Fox, who bizarrely had managed to out fact-check Boris Johnson on the status of a UK-US trade deal that very morning. It's come to something when the country depends on the international trade secretary – for the next week at least – as a voice of sanity.

For Team Boris, Dominic Raab was looking every bit like a man who won't be taking public transport for much longer. The shiny ministerial limo awaits. Gone was the pent-up anger of his own failed leadership bid. The bulging neck veins of Captain Psycho had given way to Smiley Dom. The man whose road rage convictions are now spent and on whom no one has yet pinned any unsolved murders.

This was a man happy in his own skin. A politician of hitherto hidden charm. Pleased to have chosen the winning side. Delighted his no-deal Brexit was now mainstream Conservative policy. As Amber Rudd was now desperate to phone in and confirm. When she'd said a no-deal Brexit would be a disaster what she had really meant was that it would be an unmitigated success.

This was the Sun-Talk Radio debate and *Sun* political editor Tom Newton Dunn laid down a few ground rules for Johnson and Hunt. The first of which was that there should be no repeat of last week's ITV debates when both men had talked over each other and Julie Etchingham. Boris and Jeremy nodded furiously. This time there were no women involved so there would be no need to talk over anyone.

'Pifflepafflewifflewaffle,' Boris began in his by now well-rehearsed opening patter. Optimism, mojo, complete bollocks. That's what the country was crying out for. Hunt just looked washed out. He claimed to be passionate, but he looked to be of all passion spent. The Colonel Kurtz Doll had been consigned to the toy box. All that was left was an unwanted Ken. Barbie's wallflower.

Brexit dominated the first 45 minutes and as expected neither man had any answers. But then a lack of realism has been the default position of both Boris and Hunt throughout and they weren't about to change now. Brexit was something that would happen providing you believed in it enough. What had been missing was someone who would look the EU in the eyes and tell them we were mad and self-destructive enough to trash the entire country to get things done. Of course there would be casualties along the way, but true patriotic Brits should be prepared to lay down their lives so that everyone who survived could be made poorer.

On and on the nonsense went. Both men unilaterally ditched the Northern Ireland backstop and put their faith in alternative border technologies that did not yet exist. Boris even promised to take back control by increasing immigration. Not exactly what many Brexiters had voted for, but trust in politics is now so low that no one really cares what anyone says. Coherence is a state to which no one now even aspires. Lying is now truth.

Johnson was just as confused on a trade deal with the US. This time he had at least read clause 5(c) of GATT 24 but he still hadn't bothered to mug up on clause 5(d). Details, details. Asked to condemn President Trump's tweets about four Democrat congresswomen, Hunt said that his three children were half-Chinese. Boris avoided talking about his children. Mainly because he can't always remember how many he has. Or what their nationalities might be. Both men couldn't bring themselves to say what they thought was racist about the racist tweet. That's the strong type of leadership that's on offer. Britain standing up to the US by lying down.

There were a few sparks in the remainder of the 90 minutes, but mostly a truce appeared to have been called. No major blue-on-blue attacks. Hunt appears to have accepted the game is up – he couldn't even be bothered to mention he was an entrepreneur – and is now just angling to remain in cabinet. And it looked to have paid off as Boris promised Hunt one of the top four jobs. Only it turned out that Boris's idea of a top-four job was as night porter because within minutes of handing Hunt his current job back he withdrew the offer. Johnson is nothing if not reliably untrustworthy.

Shortly before the contest ended with Boris relaxing into a few gags – his sense of entitlement is now complete – Iain Duncan Smith and Priti Patel swept into the spin room to declare how Johnson had easily won the debate they hadn't even heard. Boris isn't the only MP in Westminster to be measuring up the curtains. It will be Boris. And it will almost certainly be a disaster. Still, it's only the little people who will suffer. And Brexit always has been about collateral damage.

Exit Failing Grayling: the £3 billion master of disaster bows out

18 JULY 2019

Stop all the clocks, cut off the telephone. A low threnody emanated from the Commons benches as MPs gathered for transport questions to say goodbye to one of their finest. This was to be Chris Grayling's final appearance as a minister – not even his closest friends expect him to continue to fail upwards in a Boris Johnson government – and the mourners were out in force to pay their respects.

If you have tears, prepare to shed them now. There will never be another Failing Grayling. At least one seriously hopes not. He is the failure's failure. A parliamentary museum piece who has yet to find a job he can't do badly. No other minister has wasted quite so much money while justice and transport secretary.

At the latest count he has cost the country £3 billion in the past five years. That means we could have paid him £1 billion to stay at home, doing nothing but watch TV and mowing the lawn, and still have been £2 billion better off. Just by diligently turning up to work each day, Grayling has prevented two hospitals from being built.

What makes Failing Grayling even more of a collector's item is that he hasn't just wasted £3 billion on one bad call. It wasn't just a rush of blood to bet the house on a no-deal Brexit. Rather he has worked assiduously to squander the money at regular intervals over a prolonged period: £2 billion on the Virgin Trains East Coast franchise in 2018, £437 million on a botched privatisation of the probation service in 2014.

Nor does he neglect to sweat the small stuff, pissing away £72,000 on a failed legal challenge to his plans to stop prisoners reading books. Say what you like, Chris is a details man. A man who understands his job perfectly. To make all those around him look slightly less half-witted.

But it's been Brexit that has brought out the best of Failing Grayling's incompetence. First he couldn't even manage to engineer a fake traffic jam on a Kent airfield to prove his department wasn't ready for a no-deal Brexit and then he had to make an out-of-court settlement to Eurotunnel for forgetting to put contracts out to tender in the appropriate manner.

Yet all this paled into insignificance over his decision to offer a £13 million contract to a ferry company that didn't have any ferries for services to ports that had no facilities to receive them. That was Inspector Clouseau levels of genius. An act of extreme stupidity to which no other minister would dare dream.

All these past triumphs appeared to weigh heavily on Grayling's mind as he took his seat in the chamber. After a quick glower at all those around him, he slumped back, his mind focused on the eternity of imminent retirement. He rose briefly to reassure Conservative Geoffrey Clifton-Brown that all was on track with the improvements to the A417 in his constituency but then lapsed back into silence. As did Clifton-Brown. A promise from the transport secretary almost certainly meant nothing would be happening to the A417 in the near future.

So it was left to junior transport minister Michael Ellis to defend his boss's honour. Shadow junior transport minister Karl Turner enquired whether Grayling might like to use his last outing at the dispatch box to apologise for having wasted so much money and whether there were any other crimes he would like taken into consideration. Ellis shook his head. His client would be pleading the fifth amendment.

Lilian Greenwood, chair of the transport select committee, and Andy McDonald, shadow transport secretary, pressed a little further. It had long been clear Grayling had given up any pretence of running the railways and only the previous day he had said that he didn't do buses either. So what exactly did he do? Grayling's familiar cheek-twitch, that had hitherto been kept under control, began to pulse uncontrollably. The minister's track record spoke for itself, Ellis replied gravely. Under the circumstances not the most tactful defence.

It was more than 50 minutes into the hour-long session that anyone thought to bring up Brexit. Not because no one cares about it any more, but because there's no point. The transport secretary knows even less about the practicalities of leaving the EU than Boris Johnson. Which is quite some achievement.

Eventually, though, Labour's Clive Betts did mention that Rotterdam had brought in 100 extra vets to cope with a no-deal Brexit and wondered what measures the department was taking to offset the costs and delays of leaving the EU without a deal.

'We're leaving, twitch, with a, twitch, deal, twitch,' Failing garbled. So everything, twitch, would be, twitch, OK.

These were almost the last words he uttered as a minister. So it was entirely fitting that, like so many of his other pronouncements, they had been at best misconceived and at worst entirely inaccurate. Not even his loyalty could save him now.

He left the Commons hastily, unnoticed and unmissed, before getting into his ministerial car for a last-chance powerdrive. To wind down the windows, feel the sun on his face and get the chauffeur to burn rubber round Parliament Square. In the distance, the bells of Westminster Abbey pealed. The requiem for a dunce. A man who had bizarrely managed to overachieve and underachieve at the same time. He will be missed by me. If by no one else.

Smug, needy, desperate: Johnson's coronation is a shameless Tory jobs fair

23 JULY 2019

Amber Rudd and Liz Truss arrived together. At just the wrong moment. They looked up in panic to see the photographers were all pointing their cameras elsewhere. Professional politicians to the last, they both stopped dead in their tracks and rummaged in their handbags for some imaginary items. Glancing up to make sure the snappers had now noticed them, the two cabinet ministers started walking forward again. What was the point of turning up to an event like this if your appearance went unrecorded?

Upstairs, the Queen Elizabeth II conference centre was hosting the world's largest gathering of psychoanalysts for their biennial congress. None of them are going to be short of work in the weeks and months ahead. Indeed, there were several hundred potential patients downstairs for what was more a jobs fair than a Tory party leadership announcement.

Here in the hall every pathology was on view. The smug, the needy, the desperate, the amoral and the deluded. And that was just Boris Johnson. Elsewhere we had Tory MPs pushing one another aside to catch the eye of Gavin Williamson and Grant Shapps, who were revelling in their status as Team Boris fixers-in-chief. 'Gizza job, I love Boris, me,' they mewled pathetically. Jo Johnson merely sat chained to his seat in the second row, alongside his father and his sister. A newly converted Brexiter by birth if not by belief.

Others tried to get in front of any passing TV camera to express their devotion, while brown-noser par excellence John Hayes settled for telling Sajid Javid that 'the Treasury surely awaits'. Slobber, slobber. Javid might make it to the Treasury a little sooner if Hayes were to remove his head from his arse.

There were some absentees, though. No Theresa May, Philip Hammond, Rory Stewart or David Gauke. All soon to disappear to the backbenches. Spare a thought too for

Matt Hancock, a man who has yet to find a principle he won't betray for the advancement of his own career. He was stuck at health questions trying to explain why the green paper on further reducing the sugar content of drinks had nothing to do with him, even though it had been his idea. Hancock is very much hoping to become the first minister for obesity.

Fifteen minutes later than planned, the lights dimmed and a short video of great Conservative prime ministers was screened. Ted Heath was airbrushed out of history. Which could be the best legacy for which Johnson can hope. Then party chairman Brandon Lewis took to the stage to declare that the leadership contest had shown the very best of the Tory party. Not the strongest sales pitch, given the generally dismal levels of debate between Jeremy Hunt and Johnson. Still, I guess Lewis must have feared it could have been even worse.

When Cheryl Gillan, the acting chair of the 1922 Committee, made the expected declaration that Boris had won, everyone in the front 10 rows stood up and started cheering. And wouldn't stop. No one wanted to be marked out as the first person to stop cheering and sit down. On and on it went, with every Tory MP glancing sideways, determined to outlast the others. Competitive applause at its most nakedly shameless. Hypocrites all. We'd still be stuck in the hall if Gillan hadn't finally demanded silence.

'Pifflepafflewifflewaffle,' said Johnson to yet more confected shrieks and giggles. Given that Boris had had six weeks to write his acceptance speech, you might have expected something more than the usual glib, off-the-cuff bollocks. But Johnson is nothing if not predictably slapdash and he appeared to have dashed it off in a couple of minutes in the back of the car on the way to his coronation.

First there was the entirely insincere thanks to Theresa May – Johnson has spent the last three years plotting her downfall – then the usual glib stuff about one nation conservatism and governing for the whole country. The promises that every Tory leader makes when they are elected and are never heard of again.

Johnson then dissolved into campaign patter. People have said the incoming leader has never faced such daunting problems, he declared. But are you daunted? Silence. Boris looked puzzled. He had expected everyone to shout 'No'. Maybe they weren't quite as stupid as he had always imagined them to be. 'You don't look daunted to me,' he continued, hesitantly. But they did to everyone else. Some were just beginning to realise they had made a hideous mistake.

Then the race to the end. Pifflepafflewifflewaffle. Brexit would be delivered if only everyone closed their eyes and believed. He was going to put the E into the DUD of Deliver, Unite and Defeat, and Energise something or other. Though not the country. Everyone else was busy stockpiling Prozac and Valium. He concluded by saying he would be working flat out. Or two hours a day, whichever was the longer. His ambition is not matched by his work ethic.

In one way, though, this had been a remarkable Johnson speech. It had been the first one he'd given for years which hadn't contained any outright lies. Just the odd half-truth. Mainly because he hadn't actually really said anything. Still there would be plenty of time to rectify that. The lying could restart tomorrow.

'Boris First' policy unites UK by blaming half the country for our problems

24 JULY 2019

The Queen waved goodbye to Theresa May and sighed heavily. She had been in this job too long. As had the next person she was about to see. And he hadn't officially even started. Moments later Boris Johnson breezed in as if he owned the place.

'Has it really come to this?' said Her Maj.

'I'm afraid so,' the Johnson's Johnson replied, grabbing her hand as Donald Trump had suggested. 'You see, the Tory party have tried a hopeless leader with integrity and that hasn't worked out. So now they have gone for someone who is equally hopeless and totally amoral.' A needy, badly damaged man for a needy, badly damaged country. A man whose charisma exists largely in his own imagination.

Back in Downing Street, Larry the cat walked out of the front door of No 10 and raised a paw to the world's media. He had seen off two prime ministers and he was fairly sure he'd see off Boris too.

Fifteen minutes later, the prime ministerial limo pulled up and Johnson shambled his way to the wooden lectern. This was his big moment. The one he'd been waiting for all his life. The one he had lied, backstabbed and cheated to get his hands on. Here was his chance to make the speech of his life. To amaze and engage. But then, why break the habit of a lifetime?

Johnson waved his arms randomly in the air, as if someone was giving him electric shocks, and began babbling. 'Pifflepafflewifflewaffle,' he began. Meet the new bollocks. The same as the old bollocks. It was basically all the fault of the 48% who had voted Remain that the country was in the state it was in. The gloomsters and the doomsters had just got to learn to cheer up a bit and believe in some blue-remembered-hills version of Blighty. There's nothing more guaranteed to make you depressed than to be told to be optimistic by a narcissistic fantasist. A man you wouldn't trust to do the shopping, let alone run a government.

Telling half the UK they could basically sod off was a strange way of going about uniting the country. But then he had just appointed as a special adviser Dominic Cummings, the former Vote Leave campaign director, a man so toxically divisive he couldn't even unite himself. In any case, Boris was now on a roll. Lost to himself, lost to the nation as he failed to take responsibility for the fact that the main reason Britain was still in the EU was because he and the Brexiters had voted against May's deal.

As protesters kept up a steady background noise in Whitehall, Johnson went on to make a few mindless promises about social care, schools and hospitals that he had no idea how to fund. Even if he had ever intended to keep them. Like any sociopath who doesn't believe anything, Boris makes everything he says sound equally unconvincing. He concluded by saying he was going to get a good deal because the EU was going to give him everything he wanted because everyone always gave Boris what he wanted. Me, me, me. Johnson through and through. Boris first, second and third.

But if the EU somehow didn't give him everything he asked, then the UK would be leaving with no deal and it would be all their fault. The logic is unimpeachable. One day there will be a truth and reconciliation committee for all this Brexit shambles. Though it will be lost on Johnson as he is incapable of distinguishing between truth and lies. Just one more blast about the gloom-mongers needing to bugger off and a quick refrain of 'White Cliffs of Dover' to keep the 95,000 certifiable members of the Tory party who had elected him happy and he was off.

Once inside No 10, Johnson could let the real fun begin. The man who has made a career out of disloyalty is notoriously thin-skinned when anyone dares even gently challenge him. Now he could show his real talent. No one could come close to him for holding grudges. Jeremy Hunt would be waking up to find a horse's head in his bed and dozens of others would be publicly kneecapped. Out would go anyone with any semblance of self-respect and decency. In would come a cabinet shaped in his own image. A cabinet of shits, charlatans and shysters. One in which having been previously sacked for lying was almost a precondition.

Earlier in the day May had taken her last prime minister's questions. Almost a greatest hits show. Yes, it really was that unmemorable other than for Tory MPs, led by Jacob Rees-Mogg, who had spent much of the last year trying to get rid of her, praising her sense of public service. The insincerity was shameless. On days like this, Westminster can resemble a sewer.

May left the Commons slightly teary-eyed but she was a lot more chipper when she came to give her final, final, final – there have been so many, I've already lost count – leaving speech. Her husband, Philip, looked even more thrilled. He would get his wife back. No more having to watch Theresa being humiliated. The bad guys had won. Let them see how lucky they now felt.

Don't call it a coup, you'll spoil Boris Johnson's Big Day Out

25 JULY 2019

If a developing country had just changed its entire government without an election, we'd be calling it a coup. And if that coup had been led by a man clearly unfit for office, whom even his own family can't trust to tell the truth, we'd be calling that country a failed state. But as this is the UK and the leader in question is Boris Johnson, we plead the exceptionalism of a first-world democracy. No matter that no one voted for a de facto Vote Leave government of shits and charlatans, that is what we now have. Taking Back Control is far too precious a virtue to be entrusted to the people. For now at least.

When he had made his first speech as prime minister outside Downing Street, Johnson had briefly tried to present himself as a serious figure. Even if the content of what he was saying was still basically the same divisive doggybollocks. It hadn't gone down that well. Because if there was one thing more terrifying than Boris acting the fool, it was Boris pretending to be serious. A carapace of sincerity that dissolves on contact with reality.

Everyone knows Boris is serious about only one thing: the fulfilment of his own delusions. Other people only exist as satellites to his own ego. Useful idiots in the service of World King Idiot. A man who can go toe to toe with Donald Trump in any dysfunctionality contest. Someone who believes he is an innocent victim, misunderstood by the entire world, but who is actually a sociopath only misunderstood by himself. Someone deserving of the undying gratitude of a nation for taking a pay cut to enter Downing Street.

For his first outing in the Commons, Johnson had gone back to his more familiar default setting. The Fool. The court jester from whom no one expects the truth, so long as they are entertained. 'Pifflepafflewifflewaffle,' he began. The script remains the same, even if the persona changes. Dominic Raab, Sajid Javid, Priti Patel and the dozen or so other members of the recently appointed cabinet on the front bench roared their approval. When you haven't got a principle left to betray, such displays of craven loyalty come as second nature.

Gloomsters and doomsters, he boomed. Everyone just needed to cheer up a bit. He started as if he was cosplaying Charlie Chaplin in *The Great Dictator*, arms flying out in all directions at regular intervals before descending into the full-blown mania of Bruno Ganz in *Downfall*. Words barked out with random stresses and pauses, all designed to draw attention to the performance rather than the content. The Great Me, Me, Me. There would be endless money for this and that, the EU was shit, the opposition was shit and if it all ended in a no-deal, don't blame him. Less a statement of government policy than an election stump speech. Don't say we haven't been warned.

In reply, Jeremy Corbyn belatedly raised a few objections to both the makeup of the cabinet – lying about conducting your own unofficial foreign policy and blabbing details of national security council meetings, even if denied, aren't obvious CVs for a home secretary or an education secretary – and the ad-libbed policy. It might have been better for the Labour leader to go on the attack the previous day, but he had a lot of work to do on the allotment. It wasn't as if there had been a seismic shift in government. Or an election imminent. Oh . . . hang on.

Johnson just pulled a face and ignored Corbyn, refusing to answer a single question. This was his Big Day Out and he wasn't going to let anyone spoil it. Not so much the UK as the Boris Free State. Or rather, the Boris Free Association State as he went through his familiar improv act, making feeble jokes as he played to the crowd.

And the Tory backbenchers loved it. They were fed up with being told why the difficult thing they were trying to do was seriously difficult. What they had longed for was a clown to rise from the ashes and tell them why the difficult thing was comically easy. Iain Duncan Smith was so relieved for the change of mood that he could even forget he had been overlooked for a return to cabinet and pleaded for his head to be the first to disappear up Johnson's ample arse. Get in the queue, Johnson barked.

From then on it was all just a game for Johnson. One that he could allow himself to believe he was winning effortlessly. Just as he had always imagined it way back as a child. He even momentarily forgot he had sacked Karen Bradley as Northern Ireland secretary less than 24 hours previously as he congratulated her on her sterling work and then batted away serious questions on no-deal and the backstop from Yvette Cooper and Hilary Benn.

'Pifflepafflewifflewaffle,' he barked. There would be no hard border because Nicky Morgan had found some magic badgers to patrol the roads and fields. Everything would be for the best in the best of all possible worlds. The Panglossian vision. The UK would be the greatest country in the universe and he would be its leader. Johnson does not lie because he thinks it the easy thing to do. He lies because it's the only thing he knows how to do. This is the end. Beautiful friend. The end.

FABER

MEMBERS

Become a Faber Member and discover the best in the arts and literature.

Sign up to the Faber Members programme and enjoy specially curated events, tailored discounts, and exclusive previews of our forthcoming publications from the best novelists, poets, playwrights, thinkers, musicians and artists.

Join for free today at faber.co.uk/members

ff